# Conflict and the Practice of Christian Faith

# Conflict and the Practice of Christian Faith

## *The Anglican Experiment*

BRUCE N. KAYE

CASCADE *Books* · Eugene, Oregon

CONFLICT AND THE PRACTICE OF CHRISTIAN FAITH
The Anglican Experiment

Cascade Books
A Division of Wipf and Stock Publishers
199 W. 8th Ave., Suite 3
Eugene, OR 97401

www.wipfandstock.com

ISBN 13: 978-1-55635-970-5

## *Cataloging-in-Publication data:*

Kaye, Bruce Norman, 1939–

    Conflict and the practice of Christian faith : the Anglican experiment / Bruce N.
Kaye.

    ISBN 13: 978-1-55635-970-5

    x + 182 p. ; 23 cm. Includes bibliographical references.

    1. Anglican communism. I. Title.

BX5005 .K394 2009

Manufactured in the U.S.A.

*For Poppy and Louise and their generation*

*and*

*for Louise in her multifaceted ministry*

# Contents

# Acknowledgments

A BOOK ON SUCH a theme and set in such a context of social and church life inevitably grows out of the experience of engaging with others in those communities and the conflicts, even hostility, to be found there. My experience of Anglican churches has certainly contained its fair share of such things. But this is the church in which my Christian faith has been sustained over the years and that resilience has been possible because of the generosity and faithfulness of people in the church. Looking back over the years it seems to me maybe God had to create Anglican churches in order to sustain a reminder of the fallibility and frailty of the church. Be that as it may I acknowledge the presence of God in this "mixed congregation" which is the Anglican church.

I am grateful to Barney Hawkins and Roger Ferlo from Virginia Theological Seminary for the invitation to give the lectures that have provided the background to Part I of this book and also to the conference members for their responses. I particularly appreciated detailed comments on the lectures from Dr. Katherine Grieb. Stanley Hauerwas read an early version of this material, and his comments have helped to sharpen the focus. I am very grateful for his comments and encouragement and our continuing conversation on ecclesial matters over the years. They have come in the context of a friendship that has bridged the extensive pond of the Pacific Ocean and been enriched by the often hidden cultural differences that exist between Gothic Australia and Enlightenment America.[1] I owe a special debt to Dr. Tom Frame for detailed comments on an earlier draft on the first part of this book. Out of a generous friendship he has saved me from many pitfalls and the reader from many obstacles on the way through this text.

Long ago I read a review of a book on early Christianity that drew attention to what it called the shaping influence of "Common Room con-

---

1. For some background to these descriptions, see Trigg, *Medievalism and the Gothic in Australian Culture*; and Veliz, *New World of the Gothic Fox*.

versation," as a peculiarly English academic phenomenon. But that informal and often intense shaping engagement of scholarly academic and intellectual conversation happens in many cultures and it has been my fortunate experience in life to have benefited from such encounters with colleagues and friends from around the world. Such conversations and arguments have occurred in the Inter Anglican Theological and Doctrinal Commission, the meetings of Provincial Secretaries in the Anglican Communion and a number of other groups. They have occurred in academic and church institutions mainly in Africa, North America, Europe, New Zealand, and Australia. I acknowledge with gratitude all those friends and colleagues who have taken the trouble to argue with me with uniform generosity and to my great benefit. They exemplify one of the central theses of this book.

I am very grateful to the staff at Wipf and Stock and particularly to my editor Dr. Charlie Collier for patience, professionalism, and persistence with this project. His careful attention and astute judgments have greatly improved the text. I salute the commitment of Wipf and Stock to the great endeavor of publishing theological literature.

# Introduction

UNDOUBTEDLY WE LIVE IN times that can be both confusing and disturbing. At least during the Cold War period there seemed to be much less complexity in international relations. Alliances divided the world into two sides. The other side was the enemy and was thus evil and radically different. Each had some clear sense of where they had come from and the values that united both the nation and the church. This clarity came at the expense of accuracy about important facets of both the other and ourselves and also some critical truth about the common human condition.

While the Cold War is now in the past, this kind of radical division among human societies and nations still persists in a number of disturbing ways; disparities not just of wealth and health but of understanding. Not just understanding the elements of human life and meaning, but divisions about how that task of understanding is actually enterprised and how you might judge that you have reached some sensible and defensible conclusion. In the multiplying legitimation of individual differences, an environment still called by some postmodernism, it is much less easy to see what is common and shared.

In the last half of the twentieth century, mass immigrations have meant that nations are now made up of many different cultural and ethnic groups. Australia has become a multicultural society when once it was overwhelmingly Anglo-Celtic. The United Kingdom has absorbed many from India, Africa, and more recently Poland. For the first time in its history the United States became a nation in which no one cultural or ethnic group was a majority in the population. Similar, though not as extensive diversity can be seen in other countries in Africa. Postcolonial nation states contain groups with different tribal backgrounds. The postcolonial constitution of India tried to acknowledge this diversity and to affirm the rights of minorities, but it all happened at great cost.

All such countries struggle to maintain some sense of coherence and national identity, but in Western countries especially the fact of diversity has been embraced not just as a condition to be accommodated, but an ideal to be aimed for. This is not just plurality as a fact, but pluralism as an ideal. Such is the global power and influence of these countries, especially the United States of America that elements of this pluralist culture flow into other countries. This struggle to find coherence and respect in combination with manifest diversity can be seen clearly in the extensive macro communities of the world wide christian traditions.

It should not surprise us that the kind of struggles that can be seen in the communities in nation states should also be reflected in these trans-national church communities. The common cohering tradition of a particular church faith struggles with the different cultural realities of the nations and communities in which these churches are located. Within the nation states cultural and social understandings develop which enable citizens to understand each other and live in some degree of harmony. It is not just that there are different laws for social relations in different countries. In these different countries the way people think about issues is shaped by the histories of the country and the cultural assumptions that have become part of the national self understanding. The degree to which a country such as Kenya has shaped a distinctive culture out of its history and environment is also the degree to which it has developed its own way of thinking about some social issues. The tribal-based riots following the elections of 2007 show how difficult is the task of building national coherence.

Those different approaches become themselves the un-stated or tacit way of thinking about these things. As a consequence the Kenyan may well assume that certain principles and assumptions are simply part of their own reasonable thought world. On this basis some things seem to make common sense while others do not. These tacit assumptions thus in turn become grounds for appeal in social argument. They constitute what is thought to be plausible. Social anthropologists and sociologists refer to these as plausibility frameworks in a society. Such frameworks are, of course, not static. They change and develop in relation to the issues facing a particular society, including how it relates to other societies and the so-called international community.

Underlying the series of conflicts currently engrossing Anglican leaders around the world is a mismatch of communication arising from differences in these frameworks of plausibility. While the presenting issue this time concerns gender relationships there is also an underlying question about the significance and challenge of increasing diversity within the Anglican expressions of Christian faith. This plurality is seen by some as a threat to Anglican identity and witness. If there is diversity and thus plurality in Christian expression then does that not challenge the claim that there is one faith, one true faith? And if there is such diversity of expression does that not compromise any church witness to the faith whether that church is Coptic, Orthodox, Roman Catholic, Lutheran, or Anglican? "United we stand, divided we fall" might suggest that in our diversity we will fall and that we will also fail to witness to the truth.

There are quite important issues at stake here as to how Christian churches are to understand who they are and how they can relate their present circumstances to their Christian heritage. But the fact remains that this is not a new question in Christian history, indeed there is a long tradition of Christians grappling with this issue.

The trouble arises because we believe that Jesus of Nazareth is the incarnate Son of God. This confession means that Christian faith is an invitation to all humanity without distinction of race or circumstance to respond to the gospel. Such gospel disciples are also called by the very terms of this gospel of the incarnate redeemer, to be faithful to Jesus Christ in the particularities of their personal circumstances.

This universal scope produces churches scattered around the world in many nations. This scattered community is in a metaphorical sense a "universal church" of which all are a part as they belong to Christ. It is the living contemporary "catholic" church. It is the present expression of what we call the catholicity of the church of Jesus Christ.

The personal dynamic is a commitment to live out the gospel of Christ in the terms of the immediate and temporal situation in which we are located. This commitment necessarily produces expressions related to and shaped by the local. It is this personal gospel imperative which in turn produces diversity within the universal.

There is a very public example of these issues to be seen at the end of the twentieth century in the Anglican Communion. Anglicans, like Copts and various families of Orthodox, have a faith which was formed in a particular location and then in relatively modern times has spread around the globe into local circumstances which are culturally and socially very different from the location in which the tradition was formed. This book takes the Anglican example of the general issue in order to illuminate not just something about Anglicanism, but also about the general issue facing Christian churches.

The dynamic of the two forces of personal commitment and universal faith that lies at the heart of Christian faith creates the ecclesial realities in which the present Anglican struggles arise.

In speaking of the personal and the universal I do not have in mind the sort of contrast between universal and particular in philosophical discourse. I am concerned to focus on the universal extent of the invitation of the gospel and the specific personal response that invitation calls for. Such a focus on the gospel requires us to go back to the foundations of the faith and the story of the Anglican heritage to set out this diversity in more constructive terms in order to deal more helpfully with the present conflicts. We need a more helpful narrating of the long running story of the Anglican tradition of Christian faith. The construction of such a narrative takes its starting point in the origins of the Christian faith generally, but then tracks through the particular story to which Anglicans belong. This book seeks to offer such a re-reading which is conducted with an eye to the present dynamics of world wide Anglicanism.

This sort of exercise is always fraught with interpretative challenges. In looking back on the evidence left behind by others in our story are we not likely to find our own particular needs written into the story? Is it not likely that in conducting such a re-reading I am simply digging back into the evidence to create a story which suits my own purposes in the present? Could it not be said that such an exercise is simply yet another attempt to gain a strangle hold on the compelling issue of today by defining them in the light of the past shaped according to my interests? After all it is a powerful rhetorical device to define the present in terms of the past as construed to suit a pre-existing view about the present. Who owns the past has first grip on the present and thus the future.

All of this is undoubtedly true. The problem for the theologian, and fundamentally for the Christian, is that the past is the place from which we have gained a crucial and defining part of our knowledge of God. The trouble arises because we believe that Jesus Christ is the incarnate Son of God and this Jesus lived in a past that was different from the present. To be precise Jesus lived in Palestine, a Jew who encountered the wider world of his day through the experience of the Roman occupation of the Promised Land. Clearly this revelation of God in Christ was preceded in

4

the experience of Israel and the redemptive presence of God in their history. There was also a future in that Jesus pointed to his own resurrection and to the coming of the Holy Spirit who would lead the disciples into all truth.

The connection with the past of first century Palestine and the life, death and resurrection of Jesus has never been a merely antiquarian matter. Nor has it been an appeal which stood separated from the continuing presence of God through the Holy Spirit. How to understand this manner of acting by God, let alone formulate some pattern to characterize it, has been the enduring task of Christians and theologians through two thousand years.[1] Furthermore it is an unending task for the simple reason that times and circumstances change. In attempting to witness to this faith Christians have had to speak and act in a way which faithfully expressed the continuity of the tradition of faith and the dynamic of living truly in the circumstances in which God has placed them.

This does not mean that there is no continuity with the patterns and expressions of the faith from the past. On the contrary, continuity with the faith of the apostles is the claim of the Christian. Yet each generation has had to find ways to be faithful in their own circumstances. Not every formulation is appropriate to any subsequent generation. Each looks back to Jesus and the apostles as the touchstone for their faith and the early creeds as normative. Certainly in Anglican churches around the world the formulations in the creeds have been taken as the norm. Continuity in formulations of social attitudes and political actions has been less straightforward.

In 1848 the Anglican hymn writer Cecil Frances Humphreys Alexander (1818–1895) first published one of the most popular hymns in modern Anglicanism. "All things bright and beautiful" has been included in many hymnbooks and to this day remains among the most popular hymns for Anglicans. It is a celebration of the beauty of the creation portrayed as a pastoral idyll. Perhaps this is not surprising, for while 1848 saw Europe convulsed in social disorder and revolutions Mrs. Alexander was living in Ireland in pastoral quiet. The hymn was published in her *Hymns for Little Children*[2] and it quickly gained popularity beyond the ranks of

1. See the radical work of Henri de Lubac and Yves Congar. A more popular account can be found in Kaye, *Web of Meaning*.

2. Alexander, *Hymns for Little Children*.

the young. It lasted for many years in its full form but in 1906 the new English Hymnal cut out the third verse:

> The rich man in his castle,
> The poor man at his gate,
> He made them, high or lowly,
> And ordered their estate.

Many hymnbooks now publish it without this verse. The editor of the English Hymnal in 1906, Percy Dearmer, complained that this verse revealed "the passivity and inertia at the heart of the British Establishment in the face of huge inequalities in Edwardian society."[3] Precisely the point! For Mrs. Alexander her perception of the meaning of the Anglican tradition in a very different time and location was quite different from Percy Dearmer's, and probably most modern Anglicans. But for many years sensible and devout Anglican Christians understood the social structure of their day and found that the verse sat comfortably with a notion of divine providence. A similar story can be told in relation to slavery and its acceptance by Anglicans whose theological disposition was by no means unbiblical or unthoughtful.[4]

It might be helpful for us to sing this hymn from time to time with the offending verse included. It might induce in us a little modesty about some of the social attitudes to which we cling and which we so fervently think are requisite and Christian even Anglican. So the theologian and the ordinary Anglican will approach this matter with a good deal of humility and openness.

"This matter" is the task of learning how we are to be faithful to Christ in our generation. That task involves the life of prayer, the testimony of God's Spirit in our lives, and the witness and gifts of the Christian community and much more. But Anglicans have been part of a tradition of faith that not only has formed us but also is the landscape over which we travel in order to comprehend the story of that faith of which we are a part. Not every hill or valley of the landscape of that tradition will be important to our present situation and in the direction of that journey we are pointed to the supreme importance of the testimony of the apostles and the revelation of God in Jesus Christ.

---

3. See Dearmer and Jacob, *Songs of Praise Discussed*.

4. See the discussion in Giles, *Trinity and Subordination*.

Such an investigation quickly shows that we are not involved in simply a conversation with the past. The reality of the risen Christ in the Christian community and the resilient presence of the Holy Spirit in the life of the church show that we are also engaged in a conversation with those who live in different circumstances in our own age. In that conversation we encounter the reality of the catholicity of the church community in its contemporary dimension. But the catholicity of the Christian church does not appear as one undifferentiated whole. There are clear sub traditions within Christianity of which Anglicanism is one. Furthermore it takes only a slight investigation to see that the strength and power of Christian witness is not contained in its entirety in any one of these sub-traditions. Nor indeed can the totality be contained within one tradition, despite the ambitions of some movements. Rather each has a part to play and together they make up the whole. The health and well being of the Christian family as a whole has depended on the health and vitality of these different traditions and their capacity to see themselves as part of the truly one holy catholic and apostolic church of the creeds.

The very process of the spread of Anglican Christianity and the character of its response to the gospel in the shape of its ecclesial communities has produced both different customs and different ways of thinking about church issues. In the process of enculturation Anglicans have found themselves dealing not just with benign social and political structures. They have also encountered these political realities as malign forces against which they have had to struggle. As a consequence the personal and local dynamic in Anglicanism has created not just diversity of custom and mental habits, but it has done so at points which have been vital to the way Anglicans have understood and been committed to the gospel.

It is noteworthy that the issues occupying Anglicans have not been the matters of clerical dress or liturgical choreography that had been regarded by a previous generation to be of such fundamental importance. These conflicts really only made sense within a narrow European ethnic and cultural framework. The issues now confronted by Anglicans have to do with the way in which they engage with the powers amongst which they live. They affect not only the public conduct of Anglicans but also the character of the church's behavior in the community. Ecclesial issues arising out of the confrontation with the powers raise fundamental concerns about how the gospel is preached in word and proclaimed in deed. The acid test for Anglicans is not organizational style, nor even the details of their international institutional arrangements. Rather it is the manner whereby Anglicans can testify to the Christian truth in their own communities. That is the point towards which this book moves.

This book explores a globalized tradition of Christianity that has grown out of a local form and it does so with the current diversity and conflicts amongst Anglicans in view. This means we must look at the process by which local traditions developed and how these traditions have related to other sub traditions of the universal church. Along the way we will assess some specifics of the Anglican experience. This will involve a significant re-casting of some prominent elements of the tradition and clarifying some of the distinctives of the Anglican tradition. This leads to a more nuanced appreciation of the force of the social and political framework within which Anglicans have had to work out their salvation. It also entails showing how the imperial route to catholicity espoused by Pope Gregory VII and consolidated in later centuries took no firm root in Anglicanism. In the modern period it also shows how different political and social structures and understandings have produced different forms of secular society and different understandings of plurality and diversity. These differences have shaped the contemporary debate amongst Anglicans and contributed to the misunderstanding evident amongst Anglicans around the world.

My primary argument is contained in Part I of this book. These chapters originated as a series of lectures delivered at a conference in the Lifetime Education Centre at Virginia Theological Seminary in June 2006. The second part is based loosely on some previously published material, though it has been completely re-written and on a number of points I find I have changed my mind. In the last fifteen years Anglicans have embarked on a high-risk strategy of conflict avoidance and containment in the face of growing differences over the place of homosexuality in the public life of the church. These more precise issues are taken up in Part II, which includes a consideration of the recent Lambeth Conference.

# PART ONE

# Conflict and Connection in the Church

# 1

# Conflict and Connection in Early Christianity

T HE CHARACTER OF EARLY Christianity is shaped by the conviction that God was present in the life death and resurrection of Jesus and that this risen Christ is present in the church as Lord of his people. That confession meant that the early Christians broke out of the national and local framework of Israel to embrace a gospel to be preached universally to all people. It was also a personal gospel in that it called for a personal response of faith and was to be lived and expressed wherever these people lived. As a consequence this community of disciples of the crucified and risen Christ emerged in history with a combination of locally shaped diversity and a wider pattern of connection under the common lordship of Christ. In this sense the dynamics of the gospel contributed significantly to the diversity which emerged in early Christianity. Some differences in this community may have been the consequence of human frailty, pride, or sin. Paul draws attention this kind of divisiveness in 1 Corinthians, but he also underlines later in the same letter the diversity of gifts within the community that come from God.

## Jesus as Fulfiller of the Hopes of Israel

In fulfilling the hopes of Israel in a crucifixion of universal significance and calling people to discipleship, Jesus laid the foundations of a rich profusion of local diversity and cosmic belonging. In the second century the otherwise unknown writer Diognetus put it this way:

> For Christians are no different from other people in terms of their country, language, or customs. Nowhere do they inhabit cities of their own, use a strange dialect, or live life out of the ordinary. They have not discovered this teaching of theirs through reflection

or through the thought of meddlesome people, nor do they set forth any human doctrine, as do some. They inhabit both Greek and barbarian cities, according to the lot assigned to each. And they show forth the character of their own citizenship in a marvelous and admittedly paradoxical way by following local customs in what they wear and what they eat and in the rest of their lives.[1]

Given the manifest distinctiveness of Israel's social and religious habits how on earth did such a fulfillment of the destiny of Israel come to look like this? Essentially it came from the transforming character of Jesus' life and teaching and the creative imagination of the early Christians.

Israel was bound to God through a series of covenants. The covenant with Abraham promised the land to him and his descendents. The covenant with Moses, on the basis of God's redemption of Israel from bondage in Egypt, reasserted that Israel's God was the Lord and that his will for them was contained in the law delivered through Moses. Again the land was integrated into this covenant and made a political reality by the conquest and settlement of Palestine and its division among the tribes of Israel. The covenant with David and his descendents arose in the context of relations between the tribes of Israel and the nations around them. What was primarily a rebellious request for a king in place of the theocratic rule of God was turned around and God entered into a covenant with David to ensure the succession of his throne for ever. The building of the temple appears as an adjunct to this Davidic covenant. Israel thus became a kingdom, a nation among the nations, but with a secure covenant for the throne of David to last for ever.

Thus through its covenants with God there were four great pillars of their religious identity; the land, the law, the nation and the temple.

When we come to the New Testament all these are, to use W. D. Davies's term, "Christified."[2] The land of promise, so important in the Old Testament, seems to disappear completely in the New. The chief priests and Pharisees are reported with heavy irony in John's gospel as saying; "What are we to do? For this man performs many signs. If we let him go on thus, everyone will believe in him and the Romans will come and destroy both our holy place and our nation" (John 11:47ff). Jesus's parable of the wicked husbandmen in Mark 12:1–11 points to the kingdom being

1. Ehrman, *Apostolic Fathers*, 2:140f.
2. Davies, *Gospel and the Land*.

taken away from these custodians, and the Jewish leaders are reported by Mark to perceive that the story has indeed been told against them.

Paul takes this process a step further and identifies Christ as the true inheritor. Those who belong to him as joint heirs clearly include Gentiles. Not only is the land as inheritance transformed but the prerogatives of Israel as nation are eclipsed.

The broad new vision is laid out in Ephesians. Not only is the great wall dividing Jews from Gentiles broken down, but the gospel sets out a vision of a new humanity created by and in Christ.

What applies to the land and to the nation applies also even more precisely to the temple. Stephen is reported in Acts 7 as reflecting the older prophetic tradition that the temple had been a dangerous idea from the beginning. "The Most High does not dwell in a house made with hands." John's gospel goes further than this. Jesus is reported as clearing traders out of the temple and declaring that they should not make it a house of trade. But this reforming act is not the whole story. John goes on to record a conversation about the temple's future in response to questions about the authority of Jesus to act in this way. Jesus declares that he will restore the destroyed temple in three days and John editorially refers this to Jesus own body and to his resurrection. The presence of God among his people, formerly indicated by the temple, is now to be found in the presence of the risen Christ. Or, in the terms of a later Johannine passage, "If a man loves me, he will keep my word, and my Father will love him, and we will come to him and make our home with him" (John 14: 23).

God is present with his people in the person of Jesus, in his life, death and resurrection. He is present wherever his people gather in his name. In the terms of Matt 18:20, "where two or three are gathered together in my name, there I am in the midst of them."

The kingdom of God was a central element in Jesus's teaching. This is not a kingdom located in a land and embracing a temple. Jesus's kingdom is not of this world. Yet, it is clearly located in this world. This kingdom of God is seen in Jesus himself and in the individuals who come to him, belong to him, and follow him. There is a great deal in the gospel reports of Jesus's teaching about the character of this kingdom. In Paul's letters, the kingdom takes on a moral quality, in that certain kinds of actions exclude those who commit them from it (e.g., 1 Cor 6).

In John's gospel, this kingdom is seen pre-eminently in Jesus's crucifixion. It is implicit in the conversation between Jesus and Pilate that develops in John 19. Pilate has a material idea of kingdom that is characterized by coercive power, whereas Jesus's kingdom is shaped by testimony to the truth. The culmination of this testimony is Jesus's crucifixion. John sustains the irony latent in the whole exchange between Jesus and Pilate by noting the title attached to the cross, "Jesus of Nazareth, King of the Jews."

This great transformation in the understanding of the presence of God with his people is not expressed in exactly the same terms in the various documents of the New Testament. The gospels develop different themes and scholars have offered a variety of formulations of these differences. Although possessing different notes, the gospels sing the song of God's redemptive presence in the life, crucifixion, and resurrection of Jesus. One of the central themes is the transformation of the four great pillars of Israel's identity, land, law nation, and temple. They find their fulfillment and final expression in Jesus Christ crucified and risen. God is present with his people in the person of the risen Christ and in the company of that other comforter, the Holy Spirit.

Of course, there have been temptations to see Jesus in isolation from these four pillars that testify to the action of God in creating a people called by his name. Such moves tend to reduce Jesus to a human hero or a magical figure. The early Christians were surely right in their instinct to preserve the Hebrew scriptures of Israel as Old Testament in the Christian canon. That continuity does not undervalue the finality of the fulfillment in Jesus and the transformation of the signs of the presence of God. Rather the presence of the Hebrew scriptures in the Christian tradition witnesses to the great transformation from those scriptures in the gospel.

Manifest on every page of the New Testament is the claim that God is redemptively present in Jesus. It is emphasized in the gospels; it is the meaning of the central confession of the Christians that Jesus is Lord; and it is why the first Christians so early and so decisively saw Jesus as agent in creation and the cosmos.

## The Implications of Crucifixion

That Jesus in his crucifixion is seen as the incarnate Son of God has profound implications for any social expression of Christian faith. Humility immediately becomes a central virtue in the Christian vocabulary. Power is the power of humility and service, of love, and testimony to the truth of

Jesus. It is hard to imagine a more profound subversion of any imperial, coercive notion of power. Thus, belief in God as almighty as set out in the Apostles' Creed is not belief in God who is more powerful than other potentates in the same sense in which they are powerful. While we might use imperial images for the sovereignty of God, those images only point to a reality that goes beyond the categories of these images. The old hymn which spoke of wreaths of empire meeting upon his brow cannot mean that the lordship of God is a lordship just like that of the empires known to the hymn writer but somehow bigger and better. The sovereign power of God is always to be imagined from that lordship in the crucifixion. Jesus put in stark contrast the greatness of the lords of the Gentiles (they make their subjects feel the weight of their authority) and the greatness that is to pertain among the disciples (they are to serve even as the Son of Man serves and gave his life as a ransom for others) (Mark 10:42–45).

Crucifixion also implies the priority of love as shown in Jesus. When he bids farewell to his disciples in John's gospel, he gives them a new commandment: that they love one another even as he has loved them. Indeed this is the love that exists between the Father and the Son that is now to be given in the word of Jesus to the disciples. Jesus's prayer in John 17 that the disciples "might be one as the Father and the Son are one" is glossed a few verses later in terms of the love that exists between the Father and the Son. "Righteous Father, the world does not know you but I know you; and these know that you have sent me. I made your name known to them, and I will make it known, so that the love with which you have loved me may be in them, and I in them" (John 17:25–26).

The unity in this passage is the love between Jesus and the Father. It is not that there is a unity, some kind of separate comity within which love is shown. It is that the term unity is defined by this love of the Father and of Jesus. To speak, then, of the unity of the disciples is not to speak of comity, or agreement, or coherence, or a state or arrangement. It is to say that they love one another.

The centrality of love can be seen also in the argument Paul uses with the Corinthians to persuade them to order their assemblies in a manner that more closely reflects Christian values and aspirations. There had been some disorder in the Corinthians' church and that disorder had involved a lack of respect for some in the gathering. Given the social diversity of Corinth and the apparent social diversity of the Corinthian church, it is probable that there is social discrimination at work here. Paul first deploys an argument using a body image to suggest that each member has a role to play and that respect is due to all, especially those who might in other circumstances be thought less worthy of esteem. Furthermore, in the image Paul employs, these different contributions are actually to be understood as gifts from God. They are to be respected as signs of the presence of the risen Christ.[3] The image is primarily a snapshot. In that sense it fails to provide for the dynamic element in the presence of Christ in the church. By its very nature the image fails to allow for the kind of movement implied in Paul's exhortation at the end of the chapter to seek the higher gifts.

So Paul offers a "more excellent way" of understanding how to act in this situation. Christians are to act on the basis of love, the core value of the gospel. The various possible contributions are repeated in relation to love. It is love that validates them and makes it possible to see them as gifts from God.

> If I speak with the tongues of mortals and of angels, but do not have love, I am a noisy gong and a clanging cymbal. And if I have prophetic powers, and understand all mysteries and all knowledge, and if I have all faith, so as to remove mountains, but do not have love, I am nothing. If I give away all my possessions, and if I hand over my body so that I may boast, but do not have love, I gain nothing.
>
> Love is patient; love is kind; love is not envious or boastful or arrogant or rude. It does not insist on its own way; it is not irritable or resentful; it does not rejoice in wrongdoing, but rejoices in the truth. It bears all things, believes all things, hopes all things, endures all things.
>
> Love never ends. But as for prophecies, they will come to an end; as for tongues, they will cease; as for knowledge, it will come to an end. (1 Cor 13:1–9)

It is the presence of God in the community that will be the basis for an orderly congregational life. Why? Because the essential exemplification of that presence is love.

This is a remarkable observation. Paul does not settle a question of disorder or division with a form of order or an organizational structure. Rather he underlines the diversity of contribution by naming it as a gift

---

3. See the comments he makes in regard to prophecy in the church in 1 Cor 14:20–26.

from the risen Christ. He leaves open the full effect of that variety according to the core principle of love. Love is more abiding even than faith and
hope, and it is certainly more fundamental than arrangements of order.
This is extraordinarily high risk in group dynamic terms. In theological
terms, it is a stunning assertion of confidence in the creative ordering of
divine presence.

A similar point can be seen in the way Paul encourages the Philippians to resolve their conflicts. They are to have the mind of Christ.
This is immediately elaborated in terms of crucifixion and humility. It is
a point of exegetical debate as to whether this passage implies that God's
exaltation of the crucified Jesus is a reference to his resurrection and that
the humility was exercised with a view to, or in the light of, a later vindication. I take the view that the exaltation is the glory of the name of Jesus
as the suffering crucified one and that the glory of Jesus is thus seen in
his humility and crucifixion. In other words the passage is radically re-
defining the meaning of glory in terms of crucifixion and humility, rather
than the crucifixion and resurrection being described simply in existing
categories.[4] Suffering and humility are central to Paul's idea of glory.

Again we notice in this passage that the basis upon which the Philippians are to work out their salvation is the dynamic presence of God,
not some formal criteria. Certainly they had the model of the "mind"
which was in Christ from Phil 2:5–11. However, the passage continues
with the following argument:

> Therefore my beloved, just as you have always obeyed me, not only
> in my presence, but much more in my absence, work out your own
> salvation with fear and trembling; for it is God who is at work in
> you, enabling you both to will and to work for his good pleasure.
> (Phil 2:12–14)

The essential motivation for the Philippians is that God is at work in
them. The basis of their life commitment and effort is cooperating with
the immanent divine in their lives.

---

4. An older very useful essay on this exegetical question is Moule, "Further Reflexions
on Philippians 2:1–11." See also Martin, *Carmen Christi*.

## Implications of the Personal and Universal Character of the Gospel

Every page of the New Testament announces the great transition to a gospel that is to be preached universally and to be received by all without distinction. Paul's commission in Acts to go to the Gentiles is a story of a dramatic role reversal for a Jewish zealot (Acts 9:1–25). Peter's vision in Acts 10, and its recounting to the elders of the church in Jerusalem, is a story of prejudice overcome by divine warrant.[5] Paul's missionary journeys emanating from Antioch are an extension of the movement of the story of Acts in circling out from Jerusalem. These circular movements conclude with the presence of the gospel in Rome, the heart of the Mediterranean world's imperial life.[6] Even within the gospels there are hints of this universal application of the new Christian gospel.[7]

This universal reach is not simply geographic. It is also social. Indeed this gospel is to be brought to all humanity regardless of social distinctions. It is a gospel for prisoners, jailers, magistrates, philosophers, masters, slaves, men, and women. No distinction or barrier can affect the reach of this gospel. It is universal, it is for all.

Furthermore the claims of this gospel are seen to affect the whole of life for those who respond. Such people are new born (John 3); they are liberated (Gal 5), and enslaved (Rom 6). Almost the whole content of Paul's letters, which constitute nearly a quarter of the material in the New Testament, is concerned with working out the implications of responding to the gospel. This gospel calls for an individual personal response within the social interactions and everyday exchanges of the Christian. This personal response is set within interactions of a church community which itself is where the gospel is being lived out and is the arena of the presence

5. See Acts 10:1—11:18. The conclusion to the story is that "God has given even to the Gentiles the repentance that leads to life."

6. Paul planned to go on from Rome to Spain (Rom 16:15–28) and this is referred to in the late first century letter *1 Clement* v. 5–7, and also in Muratorian Canon, probably to be dated around AD 170.

7. There are obvious texts, such as the great commission in Matt 28:18–20, the instruction in Mark 16:7 to the disciples to go to Galilee, and the commission in Luke 24:44–52. But there are other pointers to the reach of God's redemptive providence to the nations. See Wilson, *Gentiles and the Gentile Mission in Luke-Acts*; Stenschke, *Luke's Portrait of Gentiles*; Olmstead, *Matthew's Trilogy of Parables*; and Donaldson, *Paul and the Gentiles*.

of the risen Christ. Personal does not mean private. It means the whole of life is caught up in and transformed by the power of the gospel.

The struggle of the early Christian churches was how this actually took place. In the hands of Paul this gospel did not translate into a political revolution. It did not offer a political program. But it did imply a new view of the human condition and a new set of values which Christian churches were called upon to manifest in their own particular circumstances. In that sense it was subversive.

Take the example of family structures and obligations. The gospels contain remarks from Jesus which are positively subversive of existing family obligations. Disciples are to love Jesus more than father or mother. Jesus acknowledges no family other than those who hear his word and follow him (Matt 12:49). Indeed "whoever loves father or mother more than me is not worthy of me" (Matt 10:37). Of course, he repeats the law that his hearers should honor their mother and father, and he chides the temple authorities for their corruption of the temple offerings system at the expense of parental obligations and he repeats a restrained view on divorce.[8] But the preservation in the gospels of these apparently harsh sayings from Jesus serves to underline the apostolic realization that commitment to Jesus supervenes all other obligations, even family priorities that had been enshrined in the Law of Moses.

In a gentile environment we can see a process of pragmatic adaptation by Christians to the existing social realities. A view about Christian family obligations arose only when those with social power in the current familial structure had become Christians. Converted heads of families were then able to influence a different set of family obligations by giving up power. No one is encouraged to take political or social power in these New Testament documents. Rather they are encouraged to wait with patience and to submit in humility. They are encouraged to persuade family members by godly living. This was to be achieved by living out the moral implications of the gospel, principally in the expression of humility and love.

The gospel is to be expressed in every facet of every day living. This means inevitably that differences may well emerge in different social settings. A vivid example is the confrontation between Paul and Peter over

8. See the implicit interpretation of Deut 24:1–4 in Matt 19:8, and the reports of Jesus's words in Matt 5:31–32, 19:3–12, Mark 10:2–12 and Luke 16:18.

the issue of fellowship at meals between Jews and Gentiles.[9] In a mixed group Paul cannot envisage the possibility of separate dining. The obligations of open Christian fellowship must take priority over customs drawn from their previous life, even when those customs had the sanction of the Jewish law. What might otherwise be the case in groupings which were essentially Jewish or essentially Gentile is precisely the issue raised at the Council of Jerusalem and resolved on a practical and pragmatic basis. Habits from past experience, even habits enshrined in the Law of Moses, are eclipsed by the priority of respect and acceptance within the Christian community.

Within the Christian community there are no fundamental distinctions. Where there had apparently been some kind of religio-ethnic conflict, Paul is quite explicit as to the way forward. In Gal 3:26, he says:

> For in Christ Jesus you are all children of God through faith. As many of you as were baptized into Christ have clothed yourself with Christ. There is no longer Jew or Greek, there is no longer slave or free, there is no longer male and female; for all of you are one in Christ Jesus.

Similarly in Ephesians we are presented with a vision of a new humanity embracing all. That some were "circumcised" and some were "uncircumcised" (that is, Jews and Gentiles) is clear and readily recognized in Ephesians 2. Whereas there had been a great dividing wall between these two, Christ has abolished the law that "he might create in himself one new humanity in place of the two, thus making peace" (Eph 2:15).

This dual character of the new faith; that it was universally available and that it called for a comprehensive response in the particular circumstances of time and place meant that the way the gospel was expressed would inevitably vary according to locality and context.

## Expressing the Faith in Different Ways

As the Christian gospel traversed the Mediterranean world it crossed language and cultural borders. It is not surprising that the early Christians came to express their faith in different ways which went well beyond simply different languages. We can see this process had already commenced in the letters of Paul. He wrote to people in significantly different

9. Gal 2:11–14.

social, ethnic and political circumstances. He himself was a Jew with a Jewish education and knowledge of Graeco-Roman culture. One of the interesting examples of the church embracing cross cultural concepts is that of adoption. There is no provision for individual adoption in the Old Testament. Rather the kinship connections and their implied obligations were thought to deal with the situations of loss or need that might arise. On the other hand, adoption was widely used in both Greek and Roman society and there was a clear and detailed set of procedures for effecting an adoption. Such adoption was regularly used to secure an heir and the legal procedures for adoption often included the making of a will. [10]

Paul is the only New Testament writer to use the language of adoption (*huiothesia*). He uses the terms to emphasize the "bringing to sonship" by the express and deliberate act of God. Thus, in Rom 9:4 Paul says that his kindred according to the flesh are Israelites and to them belong the privileges God has given them, including "adoption", the law covenants and glory.[11] Adoption is here used of God's action in calling Israel as a people. Paul's general usage moves in a more individual direction in line with the meaning in the Graeco-Roman world.

In Gal 4:5 receiving sonship is equivalent to liberation from the law. In Romans 8 it is the spirit of sonship as distinct from the spirit of bondage that governs the life of the community. While the terms used may be the same in these passages and the general point about personal relationship with God is broadly the same, the precise nuances of the word usage and their semantic profile is discernibly different and significant in being so.

The point I want to highlight is that Paul employs a largely technical term drawn from the cultural context in which he was working in order to express something quite fundamental about the Christian gospel. Furthermore the imagery is used somewhat differently in each case. In Galatians and Romans the terminology points to different things and the cultural significance of the terms is used differently in each letter. This is probably not so much because of the different social or audience contexts as the different argumentative purposes in which Paul was engaged in each case. This is not a novel point. It is widely recognized in New Testament scholarship and in endless commentaries on the text of the

10. See Gardner, *Family and Familia.*

11. The allusion here is clearly to the repeated declaration in the Old Testament that God makes Israel his son as if by adoption. See Exod 4:22, Isa 1:2f., Jer 3:19, Hos 11:1.

New Testament. However, the significance for understanding Paul's flexible way of expressing the meaning of the gospel is not so often noticed. It is clear that Paul uses language and ideas in different contexts in different ways. Such key terms in Paul's letters as freedom, slavery, knowledge and justification are used with different connotations and to different effect in the different letters in which they are used.[12] Furthermore in Romans, a single document in which the audience is not a variable, a continuous theme of God's relationship to humanity and to individuals is sustained using different terms.[13]

Today we might be inclined to label this "a process of enculturation." In many respects this would not be unfair. What it implies, however, for the present purpose, is that Christians in different contexts not only could express themselves differently but given the obligation to testify to their faith where they were located, they were obliged to do so.

Thus, at the very heart of the apostolic mission is a principle of diversity in relation to the one true gospel. Clearly the language of the Christian gospel is not univocal.

## Paul's Churches Varied in Style and Character

It is not surprising to find similar differences in the style and character of the communities which emerged from the preaching of this gospel. One might think that the mission to the circumcised of Peter, or James or John might have led to communities with different habits and styles from those which resulted from the mission of Paul to the Gentiles. We do

12. See Kaye, "'To the Romans and Others' Revisited."

13. A number of classical Lutheran interpretations of Romans set the opening five chapters as the foundation of the whole and despite the fact that the language of justification disappears from the text, the doctrine needs to be taken into the rest of the letter as the key heuristic theme. Schwetizer, *Mysticism of Paul*, took this a step further and argued that the disappearance of the justification terms after chapter five indicated that the Paul had set this doctrine aside and moved to a more useful doctrine of the mystical being in Christ. A more reasonable interpretation of the linguistic evidence is that the underlying theme of the letter is more general and these different linguistic expressions are used as being appropriate to the point that has been reached in the development of the argument. This has been a subject of immense study because of the importance of Romans in Christian history and the reasonably opaque character of the evidence from the perspective of later commentators. See for example, Campbell, *Paul's Gospel*; Donfried, *Romans Debate*; Greenman and Larsen, *Reading Romans*; Moo, *Encountering the Book of Romans*; and Kaye, *Argument of Romans*. For specific interpretative approaches, see also Grieb, *Story of Romans*.

not really know if this was so. However, it is clear from Paul's letters that the Pauline churches were themselves different in many respects. While it is undoubtedly the case that the Acts of the Apostles glosses over some things, and is selective in what it records, nonetheless the basic information about the social character and context of the Pauline churches is reliable enough to draw some conclusions in conjunction with material from his letters.[14] Those differences arose in large part because of the different circumstances in which they were located, the different stories of their founding and early life and the different challenges which they faced.

The Philippian Christians seem to have been gathered in house groups. We do not have any suggestion from Philippians that they were a single assembly. Indeed they are not addressed by Paul as a "church," or *ekklesia*. Acts seems to suggest that the leading people in this Christian group were socially well-placed. Furthermore when Paul left them he, and by inference also the Philippians Christians, were publicly vindicated. This social structure may well explain the pattern of conflict reported in Paul's letter. It fits the more intractable character of inter-group differences, which may also account for the more extreme arguments for agreement and solidarity in the letter.[15]

Thessalonica was an altogether different situation. The social context was hostile and the apostles left under a cloud. Paul obviously worried about them and his letters indicate a more agitated single Christian group. In this hostile environment the Thessalonian church had taken the very early step of forming a welfare system for those of their number who had suffered in some way and were in need of support.[16]

Corinth was much more complex than either of these two locations. There were divisions within the church of social rank and wealth as well as of ethnic background. They had assemblies although they appear not to have been quite what Paul wanted and they seem to have had one comprehensive assembly.[17]

The differences between these Christian communities show that Paul did not have a single organizational pattern for the churches he founded.

14. For reviews of the debate, see Green and McKeever, *Luke-Acts and New Testament Historiography*; and Sterling, *Historiography and Self-Definition*.

15. The most obvious case is Philippians 2, but see also the exceptional naming of offenders at Phil 4:2.

16. See 2 Thess 3:10f.; 1 Thess 5:14.

17. See the extensive discussion in Witherington, *Conflict and Community*.

He was not operating some kind of franchise. Rather he seems to operate on a more open and dynamic basis and to have a high level of reliance on the ordering of the community life that will come from the active presence in the community of the same risen Christ and the same Holy Spirit.

The Acts of the Apostles reports that the style and shape of community life in Jerusalem and Antioch were different again. Jerusalem appears to have elders in fairly secure roles, to have taken over a Jewish pattern of community welfare and to have conducted an experiment in common property, which does not seem to have lasted. There seem to have been Jewish Christians who differed among themselves as to significance of the practice of the Jewish law.[18] In Antioch they appear to have ecstatic prophets whose contribution to the life of the community is generally accepted. They operate in a Greek environment and are publicly known as Christ's people, "Christians." They also maintain connections with the Jerusalem church and sponsor a variety of mission journeys.[19]

While all these church communities are manifestly different, it is also clear that these different church communities are in regular contact with each other and soon develop some patterns of interaction.

We observe in early Christianity that existing social connections and priorities are in a state of flux and are being changed. The absolute claims of Jesus's lordship cut across existing patterns of belonging which have previously provided a basis for social and personal order. The immediate result is to introduce new patterns of diversity and difference within the newly constituted community of the churches. The early Christian reality was that the gospel, universal in its scope and address and yet demanding a personal and living response, laid the foundations of a rich profusion of local diversity and cosmic belonging.

It is salutary to observe that the New Testament evidence shows clearly that the issues of diversity and connectedness facing the earliest Christians resonate clearly with the present challenges facing Anglicans world wide. Every time the gospel crosses a social or cultural border and claims faithfulness to Christ in that new situation, it inevitably extends the diversity apparent within the church.

While some of the factors creating conflict among Anglicans are specific to this moment in human history, it is also quite clear that diver-

18. See for example Acts 11 and 15.
19. See Acts 13:14.

sity within the Christian church not only emerged very early, but that this diversity was created by the very dynamics and character of the gospel itself. Or, to put it another way, and to return to my opening proposition, the trouble arises because we believe that Jesus of Nazareth is the incarnate Son of God. More than that, the presence of diversity in these Christian traditions unavoidably gave rise to local traditions and thus in time to sub-traditions within Christianity. Those same local traditions also pointed to the universal Lordship of Christ and to the universal extent of the invitation in the gospel. These two elements in Christianity have meant that Christians have faced a continuing struggle to sustain a creative dynamic between the personal experience of the gospel on the one hand, and on the other the universal reach of the gospel. That is the underlying issue in the present Anglican crisis.

# 2

# Local Traditions and the Universal Church

I F THE UNIVERSAL AND personal character of the gospel created a rich profusion of diversity and difference amongst the first generation of Christians, the passing of time has only served to multiply the dimensions of that diversity and obliged Christians to find ways of giving expression to the manifestation of the universal aspect of the new faith. We can see these processes already at work in the earliest generations of Christians, and over time they have multiplied and re-formed.

The Christian community lived in two dimensions. It belonged to the risen Christ and lived its life in that dimension. But it also belonged to the memory of Jesus's life and teachings. In other words, they were shaped as a community by an identity–tradition that in each generation looked back to the historical originating events of their faith. They were in that sense a community of tradition.[1] But they were not simply a community of tradition; they were also a community led by their own contemporary experience of the Spirit of the risen Christ. It is out of this twofold reality that habits were regularized, institutions grew, and the tension between local and universal had to be variously negotiated.

## Tradition in the New Testament

Tradition is a process and is clearly visible in the New Testament. In 1 Corinthians, a text rich in depicting the tensions of early Christian life, we find Paul reminding the Corinthians that he had passed on to them what he himself had received and that they in turn received from him, the word of the gospel through which they are being saved (1 Cor 15:1–2). He

---

1. See, for example, Shils, *Tradition*; Pelikan, *Vindication of Tradition*; MacIntyre, *After Virtue*; Hauerwas, *Community of Character*; and Kaye, *Reinventing Anglicanism*.

proceeds to give a brief account of what he had preached. "For I handed on to you as of first importance what I in turn had received: that Christ died for our sins in accordance with the Scriptures. . . ." This creedal-like recitation, however, leads him directly into his own experience of the risen Christ. He then confirms the miraculous nature of his conversion and of the life of the Corinthian community. "But by the grace of God I am what I am, and his grace towards me has not been in vain. On the contrary I worked harder than any of them—though it was not I, but the grace of God that is with me" (1 Cor 15:10). This recognition of the social processes of tradition did not remove the immanent sense that the Christian community was the creation and work of the risen Christ. The task Paul had confronted in 1 Corinthians was to show how the Corinthians could better reflect what God was doing among them.

We see tradition here as a process of receiving the gospel from others and then handing it on to yet others. This process of transmission includes not only ideas, stories, and claims; it also includes customs and ways of behaving. Thus tradition is a way of seeing the present in terms of a continuum between the past and the future. The community within which this process is sustained is itself being transformed. In that process of transformation the expression of the gospel and Christian living in the community is also being transformed. In this way the process of tradition has the effect of creating local patterns and local expressions of faith.

It is apparent that at a very early stage in Christianity local patterns emerged. Paul commends Timothy as someone who knows Paul's "ways" (1 Cor 4:17). In other words, Paul has his own habits that he conveys to converts through his associates. In the curious matter of women praying with heads unveiled there are clearly agreed customs among the churches. "But if anyone is disposed to be contentious—we have no such custom, nor do the churches of God" (1 Cor 11:16).[2] While it is difficult to know precisely who the "churches of God" were, it is clear that not only were local customs developing, common customs among the scattered Christian churches were also developing.

A similar pattern of local community tradition can be seen in the form of the synoptic tradition although the issues are more indirect and the details less clear. The first three Gospels show remarkable and precise verbal agreements in some of the stories about Jesus, while at the same

2. See the discussion in Witherington, *Conflict and Community*, 231–40.

time placing these in different contexts or recording them with significant linguistic differences. The history of the scholarly investigation of the formation of the synoptic tradition has drawn attention to these differences in the three gospels, and also of course in John. In attempting to track the development of this literary tradition, scholars have tried to identify the kind of community that preserved the particular traditions and their "community theology." I draw attention here not to the reliability or otherwise of the conclusions from these investigations but to the assumptions underlying them; namely that the early Christian communities developed different traditions, had different needs, and sought to express their appreciation of the stories of Jesus in ways that were relevant to their circumstances. Irrespective of the preferred solution to the synoptic problem, this working assumption seems to me to be well founded, even if the gospels became more generally available and known.[3]

## The Universal Dynamic Draws the Diversity Together from the Beginning

From the very beginning of the Christian mission there was collaboration. Paul's missionary journeys were sponsored by the church at Antioch. When difficulties arose about attitudes to the observance of the law and its significance, an inter-church council was held in Jerusalem.[4] The mission to the gentiles spearheaded by Paul was part of an agreement between Paul and Peter, James and John who saw their task as going primarily to Jews.[5] The stories in Acts and the letters in the New Testament suggest substantial contact between the local churches. Individuals are greeted in Paul's letters, even though in the case of Romans those greetings tend to fulfill the role of introducing Paul to its recipients. Even so they indicate points of contact.[6] Paul organized a collection from the Aegean churches to support their fellow Christians in Jerusalem,[7] and the Philippians supported

---

3. For a discussion of the intended audiences of the gospels, see the recent proposal that moves towards a more general answer to that question: Bauckham, *Gospels for All Christians*.

4. Acts 15.

5. Gal 2:7–10.

6. A similar process is at work in Colossians, which some scholars do not think was written by Paul.

7. Georgi, *Remembering the Poor*.

Paul in his missionary work in Thessalonica and Corinth.[8] Paul and his associates are plainly on the move as they strive to maintain contact with the local churches. Letters were also used to sustain this contact. Romans seems to have circulated in two editions, one in the east and one in the west. The recipients of Colossians are told to exchange their letter with one that went to nearby Laodicea, and Ephesians is generally regarded as having the marks of a circular letter. From their inception, the local churches with their different styles and traditions sustained themselves and nurtured their faith in connection with other churches in different places.

During the time covered by the New Testament, the Christian churches developed common customs. A fellowship meal came to gain its significance as a repetition of the last supper of Jesus with his disciples. A practice of baptism, at first apparently not an emphatic priority for Paul himself, became widespread.[9] Indeed it was sufficiently widespread for him to assume it as a common practice in argument in his letter to the Romans (Rom 6:3), although the test is a little ambiguous as to whether all are assumed to have been baptized.[10] The early examples of Jerusalem and Thessalonica of providing welfare for the needy among the Christians had obviously spread much more widely by the time the Pastoral letters were written.[11]

During the first three centuries these customs became more widely established and firmly fixed in the life of the scattered Christian communities in such a way that enables us to speak of them as institutions. By this I mean a reasonably fixed pattern of relationship over time between people and or things. Such a pattern creates some certainty and, in community relationships, it means some confidence in what can or should be expected of others.[12] It also means that those individuals who, at a given point in time, or at a particular location, happen to have the responsibility

---

8. Phil 4:15–20.

9. See 1 Cor 1:14–17, though this is a highly rhetorical passage.

10. See the discussion in Jewett, *Romans*, 395–404, and Kaye, *Argument of Romans*, 58–65.

11. 1 Tim 5:9–16. The date of these letters depends on whether or not they are regarded as written by Paul or not. Scholars are divided on the point, but even if they are not by Paul it is unlikely that they would have been written too long after Paul's death, since his apostolic authorship is such a potent part of the arguments in the letters.

12. For a discussion of expectations in communities, see Luhmann, *Social Systems*.

for a particular function can be relied upon to fulfill the expectations that attach to that position.

This pattern of custom and institutionalization was present from the very earliest times of the Christian movement. It is present already in Jesus's appointment of the twelve disciples, later called apostles.[13] Also from the beginning it was a process that performed two important roles in the nurturing and the Christian faith of these local communities. It sustained the notion that they all belonged within the one universal gospel, and that they all derived that gospel from Jesus and his apostles.

With the passage of time the pattern of this traditional connection with Jesus was itself institutionalized. Almost certainly this happened in response to differing dynamics within the Christian movement. Gnostics claimed a secret personal knowledge separate from, and superior to, the public tradition of the church. The prophecies of Montanists came to be written down and claimed as part of the literary tradition. Marcion kept to the public literary tradition but re-defined it and reduced it to conform to his own views. Such expansion and concentration was met with an agreed list of authentic apostolic texts.[14] Also at work in this process was the impulse to find a focus for the church's connection with Jesus and the apostles. An institutional center was needed in a diversifying church.

What emerged from this interaction was a list of those documents that best expressed the form and character of the traditional connection with Jesus and the apostles; what we have come to call the canon of the New Testament.[15] With the passing of time this became the crucial identifiable link with Jesus and it came to hold a priority position in the perception of how God was recognizably present in the unfolding life of the Christian communities.

We can see this process at work in the writings of Irenaeus (130–200 CE) in the middle of the second century. Irenaeus was the bishop of Lyons in southern Gaul and was confronted with some who claimed to have a secret and decisive knowledge of God, a version of what we have come to call Gnosticism. He wrote an extensive work against this tendency which he called a heresy. Part of his argument had to do with how the authentic testimony to Jesus and the apostolic gospel might be found. He appealed

13. Witness the filling of the position in the twelve left by the departure of Judas in Acts 1:15–26.

14. See Kaye, *Web of Meaning*.

15. See McDonald and Sanders, *Canon Debate*; Metzger, *Text of the New Testament*.

to the text of the Gospels and how they might properly be interpreted. His method has many of the marks of what we would today call an historical-critical approach. He also appealed to the testimony of the church in Rome, because this church had publicly taught the Christian gospel for a continuous period identifiably reaching back to the time of the apostles. The issue for him was public testimony to the tradition. That is, that people in the wider society could see what the church was preaching.

> We have learned from none others the plan of our salvation, than from those through whom the Gospel has come down to us, which they did at one time proclaim in public and at a later period, by the will of God, handed down to us in the Scriptures, to be the ground and pillar of our faith.[16]

Irenaeus lived a mere two generations from the time of the apostles. As a boy he had heard Polycarp, the bishop of Smyrna, whom Irenaeus reports had in turn heard John the apostle.[17] At such proximity, this kind of testimonial argument could be seen to have the force of available memory. However, passing generations made it a much less persuasive form of argument. Passing generations also saw the increasing local diversity being consolidated by the process of institutionalization. All this heightened the need to find continuity in written sources rather than living memory.

## Local Traditions and the Universal

In the second century, Diognetus spoke of the practices of Christians in different locations in the Mediterranean world as following local customs but yet belonging to a supernal kingdom of God. Later in the same century a nobleman in Edessa called Bardaisan cast a much wider canvass and made a similar point. This extraordinary Christian began his *Book of the Laws of Countries* with a Platonic dialogue written in Syriac.[18] The disputants in the dialogue display a knowledge of customs and religion from northern India, Bokhare, Samakand, northern Afghanistan, Iran, and among the Celts and not least the Romans. It is a vision of the civilized world from Scotland through to western Asia that points to the distant empire of China. Bardaisan's work clearly underlines the local character

16. Irenaeus *Adversus haereses* III.1, 1. Quotations are taken from Roberts and Donaldson, *Ante-Nicene Fathers*.

17. See Irenaeus *Adversus haereses* III.3, 4.

18. Bardesanes and Drijvers, *Book of the Laws of Countries*.

of Western Christianity. It is really the Christianity of Western Europe and in the words of Peter Brown is only one "among the many divergent Christendoms which came to stretch along the immense arc delineated in Bardaisan's treatise."[19] Western Christianity is itself a local tradition within which there were developing yet more local traditions.

Local diversity was not only always present in Christianity from the beginning, it has continued throughout its history to this very day. The question at issue for us is how this local diversity has related to the universal character of the faith and how that experience might assist our own generation. Not surprisingly the profile of that relationship has differed immensely from time to time and from place to place. Three examples will serve to illustrate this point.

## Visigoth Spain

At a time when universal political connections were giving way to local and regional entities, the Visigoth kings of Spain from 589 to 711 held together one of the largest unified political units in Europe. They did this in a way that incorporated Christianity into the social and political structure. On seventeen occasions between 589 and 694 the entire body of bishops in the kingdom was summoned to the capital Toledo, where councils insisted on uniformity of religious practice in the kingdom. Dates of festivals, the form of the creed and its recitation during the mass were all to be uniform and local custom was to be suppressed.[20]

> Let one norm of praying and singing the psalms be preserved throughout all Spain and (the Visigoth parts of) Gaul . . . nor should there be any further variation among us in ecclesiastical custom, seeing that we are held within the same faith and within a single kingdom.[21]

The uniformity thus enforced was a brittle affair and collapsed in the face of the Saracen invasions. More significantly for our purposes, the very actions and words by which the uniformity was enforced reveals the resilience of local customs within the kingdom and the existence of different practices elsewhere beyond the kingdom.

19. Brown, *Rise of Western Christendom*.

20. The *filioque* clause in the Nicene Creed first appears in an interpolation into the text from the Council of Toledo in 589.

21. Brown, *Rise of Western Christendom*, 221.

A similar tendency can be observed in other places. Different devices were used to sustain some connection between the local and the universal. When actual knowledge of other local "christendoms" was scanty, this relationship was sometimes sustained by elevating local works to the status of being completely reliable sources of a universal knowledge of Christian faith. Thus the writings of Theodore of Mopsuestia were presented by the teachers of Nisibis around 600 CE to encompass the whole Christian truth. They were made into a single and perfect body. In 636 CE the *Etymologies* of Isidore of Seville were published with similar claims.[22] It is in this context of local christendoms that we should view Bede and his role in the development of Anglicanism.

## Bede and Anglicanism

In a monastery in northern England on the banks of the river Tyne at Jarrow, Bede the monk had access to 300 books, the largest such collection north of the Alps. This collection and the establishment of the Jarrow monastery had taken two generations and the extraordinary efforts of the Northumberland nobleman Benedict Biscop, who had become a monk and spent his time and considerable energy and resources building up the Jarrow library.[23] The purpose of this amazing effort was to establish a basis for maintaining a local Christendom in England. Peter Brown puts it this way:

> . . . the Christian Churches had become profoundly regionalized. Christianity was a patchwork of adjacent, but separate "micro-Christendoms". No longer bathed, unconsciously in an "ecumenical" atmosphere based upon regular inter-regional contacts, each Christian region fell back on itself. Each needed to feel that it possessed, if in diminished form, the essence of an entire Christian culture. Often singularly ill-informed about their neighbors, or deeply distrustful of them, the leaders of each "micro-Christendom" fastened with fierce loyalty on those features that seemed to reflect in microcosm, in their own land, the imagined, all embracing macrocosm of a world-wide Christianity.[24]

22. Ibid., 219.

23. Fletcher, *Benedict Biscop.*

24. Brown, *Rise of Western Christendom,* 218.

It was Bede, and particularly through his ecclesiastical history of the English people, who did more than any other person to create the idea of an English nation and to set the story of that nation firmly within the framework of a particular divine providence. His Latin work was translated in the ninth century by, or at least under the impetus of, King Alfred. In the stormy times of the twelfth to fourteenth centuries, Bede's work continued to be copied and read in England. He became, through his literary work, the teacher of the English. The assertion of the English identity and the distinctive character of their Christianity that began with Bede continued throughout this period.

In general, the English crown maintained an independent stance on the issue of papal jurisdiction in England. Even William the Conqueror, for whose invasion of England the Pope had been patron, would not offer fealty to the Pope when it was sought, although he gave respect and paid "Peter's pence."[25] There were some digressions from this practice. King John signed the nation over to the Pope in an unsuccessful attempt to evade the power of the barons, and Henry II was obliged to make concessions to the Pope after the murder of Thomas à Beckett.[26]

When Henry VIII severed relations with the Pope, he was not doing anything new. He was simply asserting English independence in an extreme way. The identity of English Christianity throughout the period from the seventh to the sixteenth century continued to form and develop in its own discrete ways. In the fourteenth century, Sir John Fortescue could draw very sharp distinctions between the English tradition of authority, regal and political, and that of the French. He saw the dispersed authority structure in English legal and political practice as part of a long history of the way Christianity had shaped the English nation and church. This was in some contrast to the more authoritarian and centralized pattern he observed in France. This period also saw a consolidation of the instruments of the nation. It became a more coherent political unit.[27] This

25. In a letter written probably in 1080, see Douglas and Greenaway, *English Historical Documents*, vol. 2, Document 101, "I have not consented to pay fealty, nor will I now, because I never promised it, nor do I find that my predecessors ever paid it to your predecessors."

26. The terms of Henry II's capitulation are accessible in Douglas and Greenaway, *English Historical Documents*, vol. 2, Document 156.

27. See Fortescue, *On the Laws and Governance of England*.

was a powerfully formative period for English Christianity and was heavily influential in shaping the tradition we now call Anglicanism.

## Gallicanism

While Fortescue's contrast between France and England draws attention to hierarchical differences between the two countries, there was a continuing struggle with the jurisdiction of the Pope in both places. The French kings also fought a continuing battle with the clergy in France particularly over the role of the bishops in dealing with civilian affairs in their courts. The King claimed to be the head of the Gallican church. Where the bishops acted beyond their perceived role, the king would take action against their temporal possessions and privileges. As head of the Gallican church the king also claimed the right to nominate bishops, to be the only authority by which church councils could be convened and also to have the right to tax the clergy. Part of the king's claim to headship of the church implied authority in matters of doctrine and religious practice. This was not unprecedented. Charlemagne (742–814) in his time had taken such a view and acted upon it. Philip of Valois (1293–1350) challenged Pope John XXII on the doctrine of the beatific vision. In a Christian nation the Christian prince often saw his role as the care of his people—"body and soul."[28] The king's claim to these prerogatives did no go uncontested but they point to the local character of the religious struggles.

While these were issues that most directly affected the life of the church in France, the French bishops and clergy had their own struggles with the Papacy. So-called Episcopal Gallicanism held not only that kings were independent of the Pope, but that, in matters spiritual, supreme authority belonged to General Councils, and popes should obey their canons. This was decisively claimed by the council of Constance 1414–1418[29] when the Papacy was divided and the Avignon Papacy was clearly subject to the influence of the French king. While this Gallican tradition held sway late into the eighteenth century,[30] it virtually disappeared as a political force under Napoleon.

28. See Parsons, *Church in the Republic*.

29. See the key document *Haec Semper* in Tanner, *Decrees of the Ecumenical Councils*, and also Stump, *Reforms of the Council of Constance*

30. See the Assembly of the Clergy 1682, which declared the Pope cannot depose kings because his power is only in the spiritual realm, and even there it does not go beyond the limits set at the Council of Constance and in any case can be changed by the church.

Yet Gallicanism as a movement of theology that sought to work with an authority not restricted to the institutions of the Papacy, or indeed fixed in any absolute sense in institutional arrangements, persisted in France. The beginnings of the *nouvelle theologie* early in the twentieth century was an echo of this Gallican tradition. This theological work by such French theologians as Henri de Lubac provided the groundswell for the reform movements which surfaced at Vatican II.[31] The Council documents *Dogmatic Constitution of the Church* and the *Declaration on Religious Liberty* breathe the spirit of a long Gallican tradition.[32]

In effect this is a local tradition that has persisted through time, even though, for wider historical reasons, it was a tradition of Christian faith that finished up within the orbit of the Roman Catholic Church and the jurisdiction of the Papacy.

Western Christianity, however, has been significantly affected by the initiatives of popes from Gregory VII to place the centre of gravity in this dynamic on the universal side and to claim exclusive representation of that universal with the office of the Pope. This is an instance in which a local claims jurisdiction over the wider universal of Western Christianity and thereby eclipses other locals.

## An Imperial Universal that Eclipses the Local: Gregory VII's Great Ambition

In order to grasp the revolutionary significance of the changes initiated by Gregory VII we need to recognize the general framework within which these changes were made. We have already seen that Christian history reveals that various traditions of the faith have developed from an interaction with the local host culture and its history. These local traditions are held in balance in the logic of faith in the incarnate Son of God. On the one hand there is the resilient call to personal discipleship which Jesus modeled and on the other there is the consciousness and power of the universality of the faith which arises from and reflects the cosmic lordship of Christ. Personal discipleship and universal connection within the church are held together in an often stressful dynamic by the power of the presence of the risen Christ.

31. See Markey, *Creating Communion*.

32. For an autobiographical account of the inside workings of the Council in relation to these forces, see Kung, *My Struggle for Freedom*.

Anglicanism developed as part of Western Christianity and for over a thousand years it had jostled with the Church of Rome and its bishop. As with other parts of Western Europe and Western Christianity there have been many ups and downs in that relationship. Anglicans, though they were known as simply English Christians, went to the crucial Council of Constance in 1414–1418 when a conciliar attempt was made to heal the problem of two competing popes each claiming the title. Anglicans have retained a relationship with the Pope that has ranged from outright disdain to respectful acknowledgement and, from time to time, jurisdictional compliance. The claims that the Pope made have not always been the same, nor have been the responses from Anglicans. However, in the eleventh century a great change was introduced that thereafter affected profoundly the relationship between the two traditions and, indeed other Christian traditions in Western Europe.

The political face of Western Europe changed dramatically in the eleventh and twelfth centuries in ways that are reflected in the investiture conflict. The balance between church and politics was symbolized in the appointment of the Pope by the Holy Roman Emperor and the crowning and installation of the Emperor by the Pope. The reform movement centered on Archdeacon Hildebrand looked to change the balance of relations between secular and ecclesiastical powers and to assert the priority of the church. In 1059 a council in Rome established the College of Cardinals to elect the Pope, thus removing the Emperor from this role and setting the scene for an attack on lay control over ecclesiastical offices. This conflict continued in the Holy Roman Empire until 1122 with the Concordat of Worms, but not before the Emperor and Pope had deposed each other and Gregory himself had been rescued by the Normans from a German attack on Rome in 1085. One of the effects of the investiture conflict was to leave Germany more divided politically because of the erosion of the power of the emperor. England on the other hand was left in a more coherent condition, and the close relationship between Lanfranc and William made for a different kind configuration of the relations between church and crown.

In the midst of these conflicts, Hildebrand, as Pope Gregory VII, pressed on with his plan to create a totally unified jurisdictional church centered on Rome that would be exercised through his control of the bishops and the clergy. The famous *dictatus Papae,* published in 1070, embodied this ambitious understanding of the papacy. The *dictatus Papae* included such things as

> That the Roman church was founded by God alone.
> That the Roman pontiff alone can with right be called universal.
> That he alone can depose or reinstate bishops.
> That he alone may use the imperial insignia.
> That of the pope alone all princes shall kiss the feet.
> That this is the only name in the world.
> That it may be permitted to him to depose emperors.
> That he may be permitted to transfer bishops if need be.
> That he has power to ordain a clerk of any church he may wish.
> That no synod shall be called a general one without his order.
> That he himself may be judged by no one.
> That the Roman church has never erred; nor will it err to all eternity,
> the Scripture bearing witness.
> That he who is not at peace with the Roman church shall not be
> considered catholic.
> That he may absolve subjects from their fealty to wicked men.[33]

This is clearly a comprehensive claim to an imperial conception of catholicity. It also provides the polar point of contrast to any strong moves to privilege the local traditions which had arisen in the previous five hundred years in Europe.

The Emperor had submitted to the Pope in 1077 at Canossa in northern Italy, but clearly this was not the end of the matter. After he had settled rebellions in his own lands the Emperor was clearly getting ready for a return to the Pope.

Looking for assistance in this continuing conflict, Gregory wrote in 1080 to William the Conqueror seeking support and fealty from him. William would not comply. "I have not consented to pay fealty, nor will I now, because I never promised it, nor do I find that my predecessors ever paid it to your predecessors." He goes on to say in the best diplomatic terms that "it is our most earnest desire above all things to love you most sincerely, and to hear you most obediently."[34]

This interchange between William and the Pope highlights a number of important points. First, that the reform of the English church was contemplated by William and the Archbishop of Canterbury, Lanfranc, ac-

33. The full text can be seen at http://www.fordham.edu/halsall/source/g7-dictpap
.html.

34. Douglas and Greenaway, *English Historical Documents*, vol. 2, Document 101.

cording to a very traditional understanding of the authority and customs of a Christian nation. The conception of the kingdom was that it was, and should be, sufficient in itself to sustain the life and faith of its people. This does not mean that it was totally isolated or that it was not connected with other Christian traditions throughout the known world. The Christian world was united in the sense that it professed the one faith and submitted to the same lordship of Christ. For Lanfranc, the idea that the pope might or should interfere in the functioning of church government within a province lay outside the range of his experience.[35] At stake in the exchange between Lanfranc and the Pope is a contested conception of the wider Christian church. The church in the West was not an empire, but a fellowship of respect in which the Pope had a significant traditional role.

Furthermore, it is not just conflict over organization to which William and Lanfranc were committed and which Gregory wanted to override. There was more than that at stake. The issue went straight to the question of authority in both the church and the Christian nation. This was a conflict that had been running for some time in the investiture controversy. Gregory was seeking to introduce a notion of papal authority that was imperial and universal in character. Lanfranc stood for a more delegated and dispersed sense of authority in the wider church, and one that was naturally expressed in a particular institutional way.[36] These were matters for which he was prepared to stand even in the face of powerful papal pressure that he should relent.

The *dictatus Papae* of 1070 stand in some considerable contrast to the pattern of dispersed power and local authority found in English Christianity. Gregory's claim to exclusive ownership of catholicity inevitably had the effect of making real catholicity harder to find and express than in the previous five hundred years.

Another effect was also to highlight one side of the universal personal dynamic that had been born in Christianity. Here was a local Roman tradition claiming ownership of the universal character of the Christian faith over against all other locals. While theoretically conceivable as a way of handling the dynamic of the personal and the universal at the heart of the Christian gospel, it did not well resonate with the longer history of Christian experience of that dynamic.

35. Brooke, "Gregorian Reforms in Action." See also Cowdrey, *Popes and Church Reform*.

36. See the discussion of Lanfranc's synods in Cowdrey, *Lanfranc*.

However, the rise of the nation as a comprehensive political unit in the sixteenth century opened the possibility in early modernity of a more local form of this imperial mode which has been extremely important in Anglicanism.

# 3

# Catholicity Without Leviathan

THE CHRISTIAN FAITH CLEARLY speaks of a gospel that is both available to all humanity and that also calls for a personal response made in the context of a community. The fundamental character of the faith means that a very extensive diversity is inevitable within each local community and between those communities. As each person and local community seeks to respond faithfully to the particularities of the situation in which they live and in which they are called to witness to Jesus Christ, the Lord of all creation, that diversity becomes visible. Yet these persons and these communities all belong to, and are called to witness to, the one universal Lord, and thus they are connected to each other. We customarily call this connectedness catholicity, a word from Greek roots meaning *according to the whole.*

The question that has faced Christians through two thousand years of history is how to conduct this witness in changing circumstances in ways that genuinely and faithfully reflect the redemptive incarnational character of the gospel.

Some Christians today live under tyrannical regimes while others enjoy extensive personal and political freedoms. Few live in nations that are confessionally Christian and where citizen and Christian are more or less coterminous although such a coincidence has been the most common situation of Christians in the last thousand years. Anglicanism has had its most recent form of this pattern in England under the sixteenth and seventeenth century *Acts of Uniformity*. It has also been the pattern in early colonial New South Wales and South Africa and in a number of American colonies during the sixteenth and seventeenth centuries, notably in the colony of Virginia.

Around the world today Anglicans live in quite different cultural and political contexts. These Anglicans therefore witness to Christ within distinctly different plausibility frameworks. My claim is that the operation of the instinct to local enculturation in the Anglican tradition has led to quite different expressions of the faith within worldwide Anglicanism. As a consequence, Anglicans in their different local situations quite properly formulate some questions of faith and social practice, and indeed the meaning of their Anglicanism, in significantly different ways.

I want to illustrate this important aspect of the emergence of world-wide Anglicanism by looking at three examples: the 1662 English Act of Uniformity, the Virginia Statute of 1785, and the New South Wales Church Acts of 1836 and 1839. I choose these three because they represent three different ways in which religious diversity within the body politic has been handled and thus highlight a crucial issue in the personal/universal dynamic in contemporary Anglicanism. They also appear very similar in terms of general language and culture when compared with other parts of the Anglican Communion. Greater cultural differences would only mag-nify the diversity to which these examples point.

## 1662 Act of Uniformity—a Pyrrhic Victory

The Act of Uniformity of 1662 is famous in the Anglican tradition in large measure because it introduced the 1662 Book of Common Prayer, which became the touchstone of Anglican Liturgy and still remains embedded in the constitutions of many Anglican Provinces around the world. However the decision to move in the direction of such a narrow uniformity was not inevitable and was the combination of a host of political forces in the tumultuous years after the death of the Lord Protector of the English Commonwealth, Oliver Cromwell, in 1658. In fact it rode roughshod over a number of interested parties and contradicted the clear wishes of the newly restored King Charles II.

Oliver's son Richard took his father's place but only for a year when he was forced to resign in the face of parliamentary opposition.[1] Confusion was dispersed when General Monck brought his army from Scotland to London in January 1660. Fresh elections were announced on March 16 and three weeks later, on April 4, the exiled Charles issued his Breda

1. See Spurr, *Restoration Church of England*; Hutton, *Restoration*; Morrill, *Revolution and Restoration*.

Declaration. The new parliament assembled April 25 and declared that Charles II had been King since January 30, 1649, the date of his father's execution. King Charles II arrived in London May 29, 1660.

The relation of the church to the state and the character of personal and political freedom had been matters of intense debate during the commonwealth period. Almost exactly the same language later used in the Virginia Statue is to be found in John Milton. In his *Treatise on Civil Power* he argued that Christian freedom necessarily involves not being subject to any kind of external restraint or hindrance. He developed this more generally known principle in a psychological direction to suggest that the consciousness of servitude induced internal servitude, and therefore to know that one was free was itself vital to being free. His twin perception of freedom as spiritual and civil shaped his criticism of the proposals to restore the monarchy in 1660, most notably in his attack on the reign of Charles I in *Eikonoklastes*.[2]

In the political turmoil of the time Presbyterians, Quakers, and even Roman Catholics, as well as many leading figures, thought that some kind of flexible church settlement would be introduced. Not only was the king looking for such an outcome but he also saw tolerance, not uniformity, as the way to social peace and harmony. In his Breda declaration, he announced a general pardon and said

> And because the passion and uncharitableness of the times have produced several opinions in religion, by which men are engaged in parties and animosities against each other (which, when they shall hereafter unite in a freedom of conversation, will be composed or better understood), we do declare a liberty to tender consciences, and that no man shall be disquieted or called in question for differences of opinion in matter of religion, which do not disturb the peace of the kingdom; and that we shall be ready to consent to such an Act of Parliament, as, upon mature deliberation, shall be offered to us, for the full granting that indulgence.[3]

When he arrived in England, he pursued such a policy of religious toleration in conversations with Quakers and also with representatives of the main religious groups at a meeting at the house of the Earl of Clarendon, Worcester House. On October 25, 1660, the King issued a dec-

2. First published in 1649, available in Milton and St. John, *Select Prose Works of Milton*. See also Skinner, "What Does It Mean to Be a Free Person?"

3. The quote is taken from: http://www.constitution.org/eng/conpur105.htm.

laration, the contents of which had been agreed to by the Presbyterians present and revised by Richard Baxter, but only reluctantly agreed to by Clarendon. The declaration looked forward to a revision of some parts of the BCP, and this took place the following year at the Savoy House Conference.

However, things were moving against the ambitions of the King. Quakers were forced to give an oath of loyalty even though they were opposed to oaths of any kind. More than that, the Corporation Act of 1661 required any municipal office holder to take an oath rejecting the Solemn League and Covenant. Clarendon was increasingly moving towards a strict religious policy. The Prayer Book revision in 1662 rejected the Presbyterian representations and enforced Episcopacy on all. The new parliamentary elections in 1662 had produced a membership that was determinedly set for a strict religious policy, and so when they came to the issue of the character of the church it was settled in strict Episcopalian terms, and legally enforced uniformity. All clergy were obliged to take an oath accepting everything in the new Book of Common Prayer by St. Bartholomew's Day 1662. Failure to do so automatically deprived them of their position. The relevant clauses of the Act are as follows;

> Now in regard that nothing conduceth more to the feeling of the Peace of this Nation (which is desired of all good men) nor to the honour of our Religion, and the propagation thereof, than an Universal agreement in the Publick Worship of Almighty God; and to the intent that every person within this Realm, may certainly know the rule, to which be is to conform in Publick Worship, and Administration of Sacraments, and other Rites and Ceremonies of the Church of *England*, and the manner how, and by whom Bishops Priests and Deacons are, and ought to be Made, Ordained and Consecrated; . . .

> That all and singular Ministers . . . shall be bound to say and use the Morning Prayer, Evening Prayer, Celebration and Administration of both the Sacraments, and all other the Publick, and Common Prayer, in such order and form as is mentioned in the said Book, annexed and joined to this present Act . . .

> And to the end that Uniformity in the Publick Worship of God (which is so much desired) may be speedily effected, Be it further Enacted by the Authority aforesaid, that every Parson, Vicar, or other Minister whatsoever, who now hath, and enjoyeth any Ecclesiastical Benefice, or Promotion, within this Realm

of England, . . . upon some Lords day before the Feast of Saint Bartholomew, which shall be in the year of our Lord God, One thousand six hundred sixty and two, openly; publickly, and solemnly read the Morning and Evening Prayer appointed to be read by, and according to the said Book of Common Prayer at the times thereby appointed, and after such reading thereof shall openly and publickly, before the Congregation there assembled, declare his unfeigned assent, and consent to the use of all things in the said Book contained and prescribed, in these words, and no other; . . .

I A. B. Do here declare my unfeigned assent, and consent to all, and every thing contained, and prescribed in, and by the Book intituled, *The Book of Common Prayer and Administration of the Sacraments, and other Rites, and Ceremonies of the Church, according to the use of the Church of England; together with the Psalter, or Psalms of David, Pointed as they are to be sung, or said in Churches, and the form, or manner of Making, Ordaining, and Consecrating of Bishops, Priests, and Deacons;*

And, That all and every such person, who shall (without some lawful Impediment, to be allowed and approved of by the Ordinary of the place) neglect or refuse to do the same . . . shall *ipso facto* be deprived of all his Spiritual Promotions. . . .[4]

This was by no means social peace and harmony by tolerance of diversity but rather the strict enforcement of uniformity. The severe terms of the Act of Uniformity lead to the great ejection of St. Bartholomew's Day 1662 (August 24) of all who would not testify to their acceptance of the whole of the BCP. As a result, probably a thousand parishes lost their clergy, representing one tenth of the whole number of clergy.

This imperial result turned catholicity into uniformity, and orthodoxy was rolled into one particular compulsory and unified regime. Some of the bishops, including the new Archbishop of Canterbury Gilbert Sheldon, supported this move, but essentially it was the work of a determined and aggressive Cavalier Parliament. This was truly, in Claire Cross's famous phrase, a "triumph of the laity."

While the laity in Parliament achieved this ascendancy over the clergy in 1662, they discovered to their consternation that they did not have unlimited power to enforce conformity upon their fellow laity. As before 1642 so after 1662 much nonconformity remained within the established

4. The text quoted is taken from http://www. eskimo. com/~lhowell/bcp1662/intro/uniformity_1662. html.

church, and the very structure of the church with parishes and freehold continued to facilitate this.[5]

The Act of Uniformity was part of a package of legislation generally called the Clarendon Code that set in place a narrow version of Anglicanism in an exclusive definition of the establishment of the Church of England.[6] Various ceremonies in the BCP and those that were now re-introduced did not always attract the support of the general population. Episcopal finery and ceremony was the subject of humorous comment, and the re-introduction of the surplice was in many places unpopular with the ordinary people.

It should not surprise us that a mere twenty-seven years later, in 1689, the Parliament was forced to pass an Act of Toleration that relieved some of the burdens of the Clarendon Code. The story of the eighteenth century in England is the story of the growing social and political challenge of large-scale religious dissent, which in the case of the Methodists was also well organized.[7]

This dissent emerged in the face of minimal changes in the nature of the establishment and the entrenchment of narrow establishment attitudes in the collective memory of the established Church of England. Such a narrow conception of Anglicanism and political passivity could not be sustained. It all exploded in the nineteenth century in the form of external political reform through the toleration acts and the move for internal church reform highlighted by the Oxford Movement and the Evangelical revival. The immediate result was the establishment of the Church Commission and changes in the legal arrangements of the establishment that allowed for some religious pluralism in combination with continuing privileges for the rump as an established church. Changes in the pattern of establishment effected at that time still continue to this day. A National Assembly of the Church was created in 1919, and only as recently as 1970 a General Synod for the Church of England was established. The twenty-first century opened with debate about the status and

5. Cross, *Church and People*, 230f.; Claydon and McBride, "Trials of the Chosen Peoples."

6. The main instruments of the Clarendon Code were Corporation Act (1661), Act of Uniformity (1662), Conventicle Act (1664), and the Five-Mile Act (1665).

7. Taylor, Haydon, and Walsh, *Church of England*, ix. This set of essays contains an excellent introduction to the new historical work in this field. See also Rivers, *Reason, Grace, and Sentiment*.

future of the bishops as members in the House of Lords of the British parliament.

Thus it remains the case even to this day that the legislated commitment to the Church of England as a state or national church remains, even though it is a shell of the former imperial insistence on a particular form of orthodoxy and a strict uniformity represented in the 1662 Act of Uniformity and embedded in many of the tacit assumptions of the 1662 BCP.

It is now apparent that Charles II was right. The Act of Uniformity and the associated BCP were not the answer to the pressing questions of his day, nor in ours. The church of God in England in 1662 was not well served by this legislative solution to diversity in the nation, a nation which still regarded itself as Christian, that is Anglican. In that sense also it can fairly be said that the Act of Uniformity did not serve well the tradition of Anglican Christianity either. It narrowed the focus and failed to move the ecclesiastical structures in a direction that served the new social and political realities of the Christian citizens of England. It externalized a church debate between disciplinarians and others, between those favoring a Presbyterian polity and those favoring a form of episcopacy. Now by political fiat that internal debate was turned into a problem of external relations. The political action changed the religion, or at least it changed the nature of the Anglican Christianity in England by changing the politics of the realm. Perhaps the best that can be said is that the 1662 Act of Uniformity was a pyrrhic victory politically, but something far worse ecclesiologically.

Across the Atlantic, in what began as an extension of England and its established tradition, a very different course was followed and resulted in a very different framework within which Anglicans were to work out their Christian vocation.

## The Virginia Statute 1785: Revolutionary Change in Religion by Changing the Politics

In 1985, a conference was held at the University of Virginia to celebrate the bicentenary of the passing of the Virginia Statute. The proceedings of this conference provide a valuable window into current work in this area. At this conference Rub Isaacs, the author of the Pulitzer Prize winning *The Transformation of Virginia, 1740–1790*, declared in relation to the Virginia Statute that "The Act for the Establishing Religious Freedom remade Virginia. In its universal language, indeed, it was remaking America and the world."[8] Martin E. Marty affirmed at the same conference that the founding fathers of America "were not wrong to put on the Great Seal of the United States their understanding and claim that this was *Novus Ordo Seculorum,* a new order of ages."[9] These may sound like extravagant claims, but we need to remember that from the first rifle shot on Lexington Green on April 19, 1775, through the Declaration of Independence on July 4, 1776, until December 23, 1783, when George Washington resigned his commission to the Congress in Annapolis, it was an epic and unlikely story, and it was throughout covered in an aura of the future and of the promise of things to come. It was the dawn of one of the two great Enlightenment experiments in nation building, a close intellectual cousin to the revolution in France and the consequential later Russian revolution.

The Declaration of Independence, as written by Thomas Jefferson, laid out the philosophical basis for the new nation in its majestic opening phrase:

> We hold these truths to be self-evident, that all men are created equal, that they are endowed by their Creator with certain unalienable Rights, that among these are Life, Liberty and the pursuit of Happiness. That to secure these rights, Governments are instituted among Men, deriving their just powers from the consent of the governed . . .[10]

It is striking that in this statement government is a practical arrangement to protect the inalienable rights of individuals. The individual is the fundamental unit in the construction of this nation. Given the more decisively corporatist notions of government and nation implied in the 1662 Act of Uniformity, it is something of an irony that the Virginia Statute should have been formulated in one of the most Anglican of the American colonies.[11] Within that general irony is the fact that one of the key elements in the perceived heritage of the Church of England in the colonies

8. Isaac, "Rage of Malice of the Old Serpent Devil."

9. Marty, "Virginia Statute Two Hundred Years Later," 20.

10. The quotation is taken from http://www. constitution. org/usdeclar. htm.

11. See Isaac, *Transformation of Virginia*; Pritchard, *History of the Episcopal Church*; and Holmes, *Faiths of the Founding Fathers*.

was the remains of the Act of Uniformity. The principle of uniformity "was in retrospect the special 'burden'—even curse?—which the colonial church of England bore in relation to the rest of the country's churches."[12] The Virginia Statute did away with such a notion in the most radical way possible and it stood both at the time, and increasingly in later years, as an iconic statement for the idea of the United States as a desacralized polity.

Thomas Jefferson wrote the draft of The Virginia Statute in 1779 although it did not come into legal effect until January 16, 1786, when Jefferson was away in France. It was James Madison who guided it through the Virginia legislature. The preamble to the statute begins with a clear articulation of the human condition. The mind is free, and should be free. That is how it was made and how it was intended to be. Thus any attempt at external constraint upon the formation of opinions is "a departure from the plan of the Holy author of our religion."[13] Further in the preamble this point is repeated in slightly different terms, "to suffer the magistrate to intrude his powers into the field of opinion, and to restrain the profession or propagation of principles on supposition of their ill tendency, is a dangerous fallacy which at once destroys religious liberty." Commentators draw attention to the deist beliefs of Jefferson evident in the background and to the autonomous world that they imply. Certainly such religious ideas as can be detected in this text do not intrude on the essential foundation of the argument for the autonomy of the individual and the subjective character of mental or religious dispositions.

The legislative element in the statute makes explicit what is discussed in the preamble. No one is to be constrained by any external force in the matter of their religious opinions or belief and those opinions or beliefs have no effect one way or the other on their civil capacities. The universal vision implied in the statute is re-affirmed at the end of the text: "the rights hereby asserted are of the natural rights of mankind." This appears to have been embedded in this statute in order to inhibit any subsequent statute that might change or remove it.

J. G. A. Pocock is right to say that this is a clear rejection of the situation of toleration reached in England by the 1689 Act of Toleration[14] and one might add the continuing polity of toleration, albeit very extensive

12. Woolverton, *Colonial Anglicanism*, 15.

13. Quotations are taken from http://usinfo. state. gov/usa/infousa/facts/democrac/42. htm.

14. Pocock, "Religious Freedom and the Desacralization of Politics," 63.

toleration, which continues formally in England to this day. The English Toleration Acts kept religion in the public sphere, while making adjustments to cope with dissent from the official religion. To some extent this also happened in Virginia. In 1779 the Virginia legislature removed the Anglican chair of theology from the College of William and Mary. Some elements of the Anglican establishment in Virginia remained, but they were those elements that created obligations, such as the provision of social welfare by vestries. Public support for the church was removed. It is not surprising that Anglicans in Virginia found their situation invidious and were supporters of a complete removal of establishment.[15] The Virginia Statute removed religion from the public sphere altogether. It was also a rejection of earlier undiscriminating state support for all churches which had been proposed in Virginia.

Clearly there are vast issues present here which go to the heart of the human condition and to the nature of Christian faith. I am concerned with this statute for understanding the nature and significance of plurality in Christianity generally and within Anglicanism in particular. I have suggested that the 1662 Act of Uniformity in England was a pyrrhic victory of the magistrate over individual religion, exemplified especially by the Quakers and those Anglicans who differed from the new definition of Anglican. It was pyrrhic in that it sought to establish by coercion a narrow religious uniformity and in the end had the effect of creating diversity and division in the body politic and to attenuate English Anglicanism.

The Virginia Statute moved in an entirely different direction. Rather than enhancing the range of the application of the power of the magistrate and prescribing a specific religion as essential to citizenship, it declared that the magistrate should not intrude his powers into the field of opinion. More than that, it made clear that religion was irrelevant to civic virtue.

The Virginia Statute applied, of course, only in Virginia. Some states retained a privileged place for religion, or even a form of establishment. But in the end the Virginia pattern won its way at the State level. The first Amendment, which embodied the principles of the Virginia Statute, applied only to Federal action until decisions of the Supreme Court extended it to state law as well.[16]

15. See Pritchard, *History of the Episcopal Church*, 81f.

16. For example, the key judgment in Board of Education of Kiryas Joel Village School District v. Grumet, 512 U.S. 687 (1994).

This did not mean that the idea that the U.S. was a Christian nation immediately disappeared. It did not. In 1843 a Supreme Court judge declared, "the Christian religion is part of the common law" of all states, and in 1892 another declared the U.S. was a "Christian nation." However, by the time of the twentieth century this was becoming a difficult claim to sustain, although as late as 1931 a judge said, "we are a Christian people."[17] A people, of course, is not the same as a nation. The notion that the people who inhabitant the United States are a Christian people is a different question from whether the state is established on the basis that Christianity is a constituent part of the institutional fabric of the nation. Clearly the answer to this latter question in the U.S. is that constitutionally it is not. The constitution excludes it, indeed any religion, as the Virginia Statute does. A claim that the people together in such a secular state are nonetheless a Christian people manifestly fails in the light of the plurality that already existed at the time of the formation of the constitution.

Before the Virginia Statute there was, of course, an existing Christian rationale for such a separation in the experience of Rhode Island and in the writings of its founder Roger Williams. A graduate of Pembroke College Cambridge, Williams left the England of Archbishop Laud with strong convictions of religious dissent and arrived in Boston in 1630. There he declined to serve in an "unseparated" church, objecting as much to a congregational "theocracy" as to an Anglican one. He went first to Plymouth and then to Salem in 1633. By this time Williams was teaching radical social views that disturbed those in Massachusetts. He was hostile to the colony's charter and refused communion with anyone who supported the established order. He was banished, and in due course he moved to Providence and the founding of the colony of Rhode Island, where in 1639 he became a Baptist. He argued for a clear separation of church and state. Rhode Island became a safe haven for those persecuted for their religious beliefs. Williams's interest was in protecting the "soul liberty" of the Christian from the intrusion of the state. The wall of separation to which he referred was a wall to keep the state out of the affairs of the church, which belonged only to Christ. It was thus a theology of radical immanence of the divine in the life of the individual and the church that led to the sharp distinction between church and state.

---

17. See Pfeffer, "Maddison's 'Detached Memoranda,'" 295f.

Thomas Jefferson made the "wall of separation" image popular, and it is mainly from his writings that it has come down into modern American discussion. However, Jefferson's most famous use of the image is in his letter to members of the Danbury Baptist Association in 1802:

> Believing with you that religion is a matter which lies solely be-
> tween man and his God, that he owes account to none other for
> his faith or his worship, that the legislative powers of government
> reach actions only, and not opinions, I contemplate with sovereign
> reverence that act of the whole American people which declared
> that their legislature should "make no law respecting an establish-
> ment of religion, or prohibiting the free exercise thereof," thus
> building a wall of separation between church and State.[18]

The net result turns out to be much the same whether you concen-
trate religion in the private domain directly, or exclude it from the public
domain and thus leave it by default only in the private. It is thus not surprising that David Little can show that Williams's conclusions on civic
virtue are entirely consonant with those of Jefferson in both the Virginia
Statute and in his Memorial and Remonstrance.[19]

There are key issues at stake here about power. The magistrate's
power is the power of coercion in relation to actions. It has no relevance
to private opinions or convictions, religious or otherwise. The Statute has
scope not only for religious experience or views, but for any kind of personal convictions or views. Thus it places democracy before philosophy.[20]

For the Christian, however, it raises some very complicated questions about the nature of Christ's lordship. A secular, or de-sacralized,
magistrate will always resist any institutional presence of an alternative supreme power. We can see this at work in Book IV of Jean Jacque
Rousseau's *Social Contract*, an author not far distant in sentiments from
the Virginia Statute.[21] Having established a state on the basis of a social
contract between individuals for whom knowledge is immediately and
authoritatively obtained from nature and not from any human tradition
or external habits, Rousseau wished to rule out any presence of a religious
power in the state on the grounds that it represented an alien force in

18. Thomas Jefferson, letter to the Danbury Baptist Association, January 1, 1802; from Peterson, *Thomas Jefferson Writings*, 510.

19. Little, "Religion and Civil Virtue in America," 237–56.

20. See Rorty, "Priority of Democracy to Philosophy," 257–83.

21. Rousseau and Gourevitch, *Social Contract*.

the new enlightened secular state.[22] Rousseau probably had in mind the Jesuits. But in Revolutionary America the particularly focused institution of religious authority was Anglican episcopacy and thus the principal target was the established position of the Anglican Church.

Rousseau's strategy was to ban the propagators of such views from the community. The Virginia Statute's strategy was to remove these views from any place in public life. In the Virginia Statute therefore the magistrate trumps any kind of Christendom-version of Jesus Christ in the arena of public or civic action, and it does so in the name of the natural rights of the individual. Pocock makes the point in relation to the Pentecostal sects:

> But when the Pentecostal sects talk of remaking liberal society in Christ's image, the statute and its progeny are there to tell them that this is only bluster; their kingdom is not of this world. The secular magistrate retains his position as the best guarantor of a free society, and has not ceased trying to remake religion according to his own specifications.[23]

This quotation brings together two important and related issues. On the one hand, the lordship of Christ is excluded from the public arena. Thus the claim of the cosmic lordship of Christ becomes a matter of private opinion, even though it might be shared by a number of people, even a large number of people. However, in order to secure this position the magistrate must seek to remake religion so that it suits his dominance in the public arena. A radical change in politics of this kind implies a change in the nature of religion.

Stephen Carter has pointed out that the wall of separation image is used in modern America to the opposite effect of that found in Williams and Jefferson. In the earlier instances the wall is to keep the state out of religion. In the modern debate it is used to keep religion out of the state.[24] He also argues that "the antiestablishment provision in the First Amendment was included *solely* to prevent the Congress from establishing a national church or interfering with those states that had established churches."[25]

22. See the discussion in Barth, *Protestant Theology*, 77–79.

23. Pocock, "Religious Freedom," 70.

24. Carter, *God's Name in Vain,* 74–79.

25. Ibid., 217n21.

Roger Willliams did have views on the role of the state and was at times politically active. However his real interest was in protecting the "soul liberty" of the Christian. That meant in principle the "soul liberty" of any individual. Thus Jews found a friendly home in Rhode Island. Jefferson's interests may not have been so religiously directed, though the text through which his "wall of separation" imagery is best known is addressed to Baptists whose interests were certainly the protection of their individual consciences. The reality is that once such a separation is in place the degree to which it is seen to protect one interest or another will depend on the perspective of those concerned at the time. It provides for ample rhetorical material for any battle of standing.

The question then becomes how is the cosmic lordship of Christ made manifest, or at least attested to. It is at this point that the Anglican tradition begins to make some distinctions that are reasonably important in our present situation. In Book IX of his *Laws of Ecclesiastical Polity*, Richard Hooker makes a distinction between the lordship of Christ and the lordship of the king.[26] The lordship of the king is limited to material things, in much the same way that we see in the Virginia Statute. The Lordship of Christ is more intensive and reaches to the inner world of human experience, of spirit and thought. The lordship of the king reaches only to the extent of his kingdom, that of Christ is universal both in its locational extent and through time. These lordships are not mutually exclusive alternatives but the lordship of Christ is clearly superior and is both public and private. The lordship of Christ thus represents the universal and personal character of the gospel by which this lordship is effected.

If that is so, then what would that lordship of Christ look like in the life of the church? The New Testament is full of references to this question. The pre-eminent character of church life that manifests this lordship of Christ is love. Not any kind of love, but love that is shown to be the love of God by the incarnate life of Jesus Christ. Paul speaks of the fruits of the Spirit in Gal 5:22, which are set in contrast to the works of the flesh. They include "love, joy, peace, patience, kindness, generosity, faithfulness, gentleness and self control." These are not set out as a moral code but as exemplifications of the effectual working of the Spirit in the life of the church. That way of speaking makes it impossible to speak of

26. See Hooker, *Works of Richard Hooker*; and the discussion of this material in McGrade, "Coherence of Hooker's Polity"; and Kaye, *Reinventing Anglicanism*, 102–23.

the kingdom of Christ in simply moral terms, nor yet in simply amoral spiritual terms.

This means that the church becomes the arena for the manifestation of the character of the kingdom of Christ.[27] Here is a community where there is clearly a transcendental cohering framework that applies not just to individuals in their private opinions, but to their public and visible lives. Such a religion is not explicitly excluded from the terms of the Virginia Statute, but it is certainly not encouraged. The assumptions and the tendencies move the notion of religion into a more internal and invisible place.

The nature of a cohering civic virtue in the United States has been and remains a vigorously debated matter. One dominant theme is that the effect of the logic of the Virginia Statute has been to move the quest for any cohering civic virtue from the content of any proposal in the direction of the process by which a proposal is promoted and agreed.[28] Civic virtue thus becomes a matter of ceaseless and continuing negotiation with a set of traditional assumptions that privilege the individual. Such an environment would very likely tend to multiply religions and religious groupings and mute the dissenting and alien character of the church by making it just one market outlet among many offering products for private consumption.

This phenomenon in the U.S. is deeply ambiguous for the Christian and for the church, and it is especially so for Anglicans who are the heirs of a tradition of Christianity that has within it a clear history of engagement with the political life of the community. That engagement had been formed within the framework of assumptions about the character of England as a Christian nation in which church and state were coterminous. The transition that overtook this Christian nation in the nineteenth century had the effect of changing the framework of assumptions about the character and basis of social life while maintaining sufficient appearance of the Christian nation as to make those fundamental changes easily

27. This has been the theme of a number of works by Stanley Hauerwas, most notably in *Community of Character*; see also Hauerwas, Berkman, and Cartwright, *Hauerwas Reader*.

28. Due process is embedded in the U.S. constitution in relation to the federal government in the Fifth Amendment: "No person shall be . . . deprived of life, liberty, or property, without due process of law. . . ." and in relation to the states in the Fourteenth Amendment.

overlooked. In the case of the U.S., that dramatic transition began with the Virginia Statute and the understanding of the nation as built upon the enlightenment notions of individuality. Stanley Hauerwas draws attention to the widespread acceptance by Christians in the U.S. of notions of justice, the nation, and freedom of religion and that these have become part of the way in which Christians in the U.S. understand their role and the role of the churches in American society. Yet he contends that "the current emphasis on justice and rights as the primary norms guiding the social witness of Christians is in fact a mistake."[29] The argument turns on the way in which such concepts arise from Enlightenment assumptions and are thus shaped in categories alien to Christian assumptions.

If the account offered here of the effects of the cultural mentality of the Virginia Statue and the multiplicity of denominations is anywhere near the truth, then it would appear that these social and cultural influences have moved the church in a similar direction to that of the broader society. This means that the engagement of Christians and the churches with such a culture is not at all straightforward. One might find it hard to resist the conclusion that changing the politics, as the Virginia Statute did, has had the effect also of reshaping the character of religion.[30] The direction of this movement is in general terms in the opposite direction to that which we have noticed in England. There the starting base of a Christian nation has not been explicitly rejected in the decisive way that we see in the Virginia Statute. Yet the challenge for the Christian and for the church to live Christianly in such societies remains similarly ambiguous and challenging, even though the terms of that challenge are set in different particular terms.

## The New South Wales Church and the Collapse of the Anglican State

These issues appear also in Australia, though the cultural assumptions and the particular form of the challenge are different.

Just as the various colonies in America were founded for a variety of reasons, so too in Australia British colonies were founded as differ-

29. Hauerwas, *After Christendom*, 46.

30. See the interesting discussion of the difficulties involved in Carter, *Culture of Disbelief* and *Dissent of the Governed*.

ent kinds of settlements.[31] New South Wales was established as a jail in 1788, with some free settlers to provide infrastructure services, and so was Tasmania in 1803. Victoria on the other hand was founded on the basis of illegal private enterprise in 1835. South Australia began as a government-sponsored private enterprise settlement in 1836. All of these Colonies were given representative self-government in 1850 by the Australian Constitutions Act. Queensland began in 1824 as a branch penal colony of NSW but later was given over to free settlers. It was made a separate colony in 1859 with representative self-government. Western Australia began as a free settlers colony in 1829, later became a depository for convicts from Britain until 1842 and in 1889 became a self-governing colony. Up until 1850 NSW, with limited local legislative powers, was the principal authority in Australia.[32]

In NSW, the Church of England was the sole ecclesiastical presence with a chaplain operating under the articles of war. In 1824 an archdeacon was appointed who had his own court and registry and ranked second in the colony after the governor. He had executive authority for all ecclesiastical activity. There were by now other churches present, but they were in a dependent position. For example, all marriages had to go through the Anglican archdeacon's registry. In 1828 one seventh of all crown land in Australia was given over to the Church and Schools Corporation, a body set up to provide support for the Anglican Church in the colony. On the basis of such munificence, Archdeacon Thomas Scott developed plans for a scheme of primary and secondary schools and a university. To all intents and purposes Anglicanism was the established church in NSW and received extensive government support.[33]

But in the 1820s free settlers began arriving in greater numbers, the colony prospered commercially, other churches began to function, and demands for a more equitable treatment of the churches began to be voiced. In 1829 Roman Catholic emancipation was enacted in England,

31. Davison, *Oxford Companion to Australian History*; Kociumbas, *Oxford History of Australia*; Inglis, *Australian Colonists*; and Atkinson, *Europeans in Australia*.

32. On the constitutional developments, see Lumb, *Constitutions of the Australian States*.

33. There is some debate as to whether, strictly speaking, the Church of England was ever established in New South Wales. At the time more was assumed than articulated. See Young, "Church and State in the Legal Tradition of Australia"; Daw, *Church and State in the Empire* and "Church and State in the Empire"; Lane, *Australian Federal System*; and Ward, *State and the People*.

and in the same year William Grant Broughton came to NSW as the new archdeacon. Broughton was a high churchman. Because he was more politically astute than his predecessor he was able to sustain the Anglican ascendancy more effectively against the rising tide of opposition. The arrival of Richard Bourke as the new governor in 1831 changed the balance, and it soon became obvious that Broughton was engaged in a rearguard action to defend the Anglican position. The Church and Schools Corporation was abolished in 1833.[34]

1836 was a big year for Broughton. He was made the first, and as it turned out, the only, Bishop of Australia. When he returned from England he was confronted with Richard Bourke's new Church Act. This act swept away the privileged position of the Anglican Church and provided financial aid to all churches on a pro rata basis and in relation to the ability of the church to raise funds. Broughton appeared to acquiesce in the face of this Act, not least because he could see that the Imperial Government was in favor of it and would support the kind of measures involved. He also recognized that he would do very nicely out of the proposed financial support from the Government treasury at a time when he was seriously in need. He took the money and decided to establish what he called a church citadel and to wait for better times.[35]

However, when it came to education Broughton took a very different approach.[36] In 1839 the Governor introduced a proposal to do away with the government-subsidized church schools and establish government schools in which the Bible would be taught. This was called the British and Foreign school system.

The proposal elicited a lengthy speech from Broughton before the Legislative Council in which he set out his understanding of the constitutional position to which he said the Governor was committed. He declared that the constitution united church and state. Therefore the Church of England had a right to expect "the fullest measure of aid and encouragement." Recent toleration acts in England did not change that

34. For a general account of the story of Anglicanism in Australia, see Frame, *Anglicans in Australia*; Kaye, *Anglicanism in Australia*; and an interpretative narrative in Kaye, *Reinventing Anglicanism*, 12–46.

35. See Shaw, *Patriarch and Patriot*, chapter 7; and Austin, *Australian Education, 1788–1900*.

36. Bridge, "Review Essay"; and Shaw, *Patriarch and Patriot*, 128–34.

essential element in the constitution. In relation to those who conducted the Glorious Revolution of 1688 he said:

> The object which they had in view, was to ensure the possession of truth and the enjoyment of liberty to the subjects of Britain; and their reason for connecting the throne so inseparably with this faith, was their persuasion, that this faith was most consonant with truth and most friendly to liberty. And I must say, that if we, abandoning their principles, should ever be induced to legislate upon the assumption, that exclusive privileges have necessarily the tendency and the termination which Your Excellency imputes to them, and that men have such absolutely equal rights, that these are infringed whensoever any privilege is established, which does not extend to all and is not approved by all, I am tolerably certain that, though the application of this may begin with the church, it will not finish with it; but we shall find that, instead of resting under the shade of monarchy, we are fast advancing, and even far advanced, towards the institutions of a republic; and I greatly fear also a republic without religion.[37]

It would be difficult to find a clearer statement of the Anglican establishment mindset that incorporated toleration into the body politic without changing anything else. It is in the sharpest contrast with the tenor of the Virginia Statute on a number of fronts. It is determined to retain not just religion, but Anglicanism, as essential to the profession of the state. Furthermore, this rationale gives no place to inalienable individual rights as a basis for polity. On the contrary, this is a communitarian conception of the state. Its qualities and fundamental principles begin with the tradition of order and institutions that have evolved over time, of which the Glorious Revolution of 1688 was but a notable change in a long line of continuity.[38]

Broughton's objections, together with his petitions that showed at least that many people wanted to keep a comprehensive system of exclusively church schools, carried the day. A decade passed before the govern-

37. Broughton, *Speech of the Lord Bishop*, 12–13.

38. Broughton had long regarded this period of history as extremely significant. After reading the history of Charles II by Harris during his voyage to Australia, he noted in his journal on June 5, "Of all periods whereof the history has been written I consider this as the most deeply interesting, and it is one concerning which all Englishmen ought to have their minds well made up," Broughton, *Diary Kept during the Voyage*. The book he was reading was almost certainly Harris, *Historical and Critical Account*.

ment started their own state schools, which began to teach the Bible and what came to be called non-dogmatic Christianity. In 1880 the government established its own comprehensive system of schools and eliminated all subsidies to church schools. These schools were all to teach general religious education, including the Bible, and clergy from the churches were to have reserved time on the timetable to come into the school to teach their own church doctrines. This was called free, compulsory, and secular. It was not quite free in NSW because parents paid a small fee. But it was compulsory. It was also secular in the sense that it was not controlled by any church rather than that it excluded religion. On the contrary the curriculum was certainly religious, indeed Christian. Anglicans entered into this scheme and retained only a small number of their schools on a private basis. The Roman Catholic Church refused to join and set about establishing its own parish school system.

This conception of "secular" can be found throughout the nineteenth century in legal and institutional understandings of Australian society. The first university in Australia, the University of Sydney, was founded on such principles. It was to be secular in that it was not controlled by the institutional churches. The opening preamble to the Act establishing the University states "Whereas it is deemed expedient for the better advancement of religion and morality, and the promotion of useful knowledge. . . ." This element remains in the charter of the University to this day.[39]

These were the principles that shaped the mid-nineteenth century in NSW when most of the important social institutions were established. The foundational character of this society was thus clearly communitarian in the sense that it envisaged a community that had a distinct character, and its version of humanity was shaped by the civic virtues that its founding tradition laid out. An important part of that influence had an Anglican flavor.[40]

These values are clearly different from those embodied in the Virginia Statute, and they are also different from those in the residual establishment of the Church of England. They represent a view that there is such a thing as general Christianity and that this is a Christian society in that sense. It was this general Christianity that the government schools were

39. See Cable, "Religious Controversies in New South Wales," and "The University of Sydney and Its Affiliated College, 1850–1880." There is now an institutional history of the University of Sydney. Turney, *Australia's First*.

40. Fletcher, "Anglicanism and Nationalism."

to teach. The assumption that the religion of the society was to all intents and purposes Christian in this sense remained throughout the nineteenth century and well into the twentieth. The fact that there were non-Christian religions represented within the community whose members supposedly enjoyed every civil liberty did not affect this assumption until well into the twentieth century, when it was modified but not eliminated by federal legislation on multiculturalism.

The Commonwealth constitution enacted in 1901 contains a clause on religion similar to that found in the U.S. First Amendment. However there is a critical difference that has had quite an influence on the interpretation of the clause by the High Court of Australia. In the Australian constitution, clause 116 provides that the Commonwealth will make no provision for the establishment of "any" religion.[41] The High Court has consistently interpreted the clause to mean any particular religion. Thus in the Australian context there is a legal principle of equitable entanglement, in contrast to the U.S. principle of non-entanglement. Similarly, Australia does not have any absolute sense of a separation of church and state such as prevails in the United States.[42]

Given that Australia has a very strong common-law legal tradition, these early formulations have a continuing influence on the way the society operates and the way habits and judgments are formed.

## Universal and Personal in a Current of Conscious Plurality

I have taken these three examples in order to provide some flesh to the point that within the Anglican Communion there are some very significant differences in the way local communities understand themselves, and thus how they approach the meaning of Anglicanism. I have not

41. The text of the First Amendment that was ratified on December 15, 1791, is "Congress shall make no law respecting an establishment of religion, or prohibiting the free exercise thereof; or abridging the freedom of speech, or of the press; or the right of the people peaceably to assemble, and to petition the Government for a redress of grievances." The text of clause 119 of the Australian Constitution which came into effect July 9, 1900, is: "The Commonwealth shall not make any law for establishing any religion, or for imposing any religious observance, or for prohibiting the free exercise of any religion, and no religious test shall be required as a qualification for any office or public trust under the Commonwealth." See Kaye, "Australian Definition of Religion."

42. Cumbrae-Stewart, "Section 116 of the Constitution"; Evans, *Interpreting the Free Exercise of Religion*; Ely, *Unto God and Caesar*; and Frame, *Church and State*.

dealt exhaustively with each situation, but in general those parts of the Anglican Communion that derived from the British Empire tend to have societal foundations similar to that prevailing in Australia. In Africa this is reinforced by indigenous cultures that tend to be communitarian. Those parts of the Anglican Communion established by the missionary activity of ECUSA tend to follow a little more the American tradition.

In all three of these examples the starting point was an Anglican establishment. But history has produced strikingly different positions in these countries for Anglicans. In broad, sweeping terms the situation in each country is somewhat as follows on the issues of establishment, toleration, rights, civic virtue, entanglement, and the basis of civic virtue:

In England there is a residual Anglican Church establishment, wide religious toleration, and no bill of rights until 2005, when the bill of rights from the European Union was incorporated into British law. There is accepted religious influence on the public formation of civic virtue, deep state entanglement with the Church of England, less with others, and a modified communitarian plurality.[43]

In the United States of America there is a deliberate removal of religious establishment, complete religious toleration, and a constitution based on inalienable individual rights. Religion is in principle excluded from the definition of public civic virtue. There is a legal doctrine of non-entanglement, and an individualist, pluralist society. It ought not to be surprising that religious language is very widely used in politics in the United States. The very fact that so many Americans are religiously committed makes it inevitable that the language of religion will be used by politicians in the practice of their persuasive arts. We will need to come back to this issue in more detail in the next chapter.

In Australia there is a deliberate removal of any Anglican establishment in favor of a possible, equitable establishment, wide religious toleration, a common-law (that is, a tradition) basis of rights and duties, and no inalienable individual rights established in the constitution. General Christianity or religion is part of public civic rights formation; there is equitable state entanglement with churches and a modified communitarian plurality.[44]

43. This, despite the best efforts of Margaret Thatcher. See Kingdom, *No Such Thing as Society?*

44. For an elaboration of the difference made by the timing of the founding of the European settlement in Australia, see Trigg, *Medievalism and the Gothic*. The older

In every one of these cases Anglicans have collaborated or acquiesced in these different social and cultural contexts. Furthermore they have done so in no small degree because of an enculturating impulse within their own religious tradition. We are faced then with the fascinating situation that Anglicans, out of the impulses of their own tradition, have responded to their local circumstance in such a way that they have contributed to the creation of significantly different frameworks in which they now seek to fulfill their Anglican vocation as Christians.

This means that they approach some of the common human questions in quite different ways. This is because they are influenced by their immediate context and because their first responsibility is to their neighbors in that local context. So it is not simply that the Anglican Church of Australia or other provinces in the Anglican Communion are more conservative than ECUSA on gender relationships issues for instance. The reality is that they actually approach the question differently. They accept different assumptions about the human condition. They bring socially formed assumptions from their own context, which shape the way they think about specific issues. For example, on the issue of gay and lesbian people in the church, Americans come to this question powerfully influenced by assumptions about individual human rights, whereas in Australia that aspect of the debate has been significantly muted. In Nigeria such assumptions are even more different.

The problem is that the Christian obligation to respond to the gospel in the terms of our circumstances means that differences arise between local traditions, and these differences create challenges of sustaining connection with others. The trouble arises because we believe in the incarnation of the Son of God in the person of Jesus of Nazareth. The declaration of the universal cosmic truth about God in the particular circumstances of first-century Palestine laid down a tension for the Christian community. The tension is how to be faithful in the local circumstances of our lives and remain also effectively connected to others in the religion.

Of course these contrasts are modified by global interactions and cultural commonalities. Also in each different location there is argument, or at lest difference of opinion, as to how far enculturation can go before it becomes a matter of "being conformed to this world" and even whether these are the appropriate terms to work with. But at root the fact remains

---

standard text on the fragment theory of founding colonies is Hartz, *Founding of New Societies.*

that in different locations Anglicans approach such questions within different frameworks and plausibility structures.

One important consequence of this is that communication between these different localities at any profound level is not straightforward and takes a lot of time and listening. It also means that the establishment on a global basis of common attitudes or policies on some issues, and the creation of institutional arrangements to express them, is clearly a deeply ambiguous matter.

# 4

# The Powers, Church, and Truth

THE PRESENT CRISIS IN worldwide Anglicanism is about how people can relate to each other positively within the church while differing on issues each regards as profoundly important. As a consequence the unity of the church and the identity of Anglicanism have become central themes in the public arguments. In these conflicts unity often is taken to mean agreement, and Anglican identity is sought as the core around which we can agree. In the previous three chapters I have argued that there is another background to this situation, a background that has its origins in the very character of the gospel. The confession that Jesus is Lord meant that the gospel invitation was open to all without distinction and further that each was called to respond personally. This personal response to the gospel must lead to a new life in Christ set in the day-to-day circumstances in which the believer lived. As a result, there emerged a community of disciples of Christ in which could be found locally shaped diversity. This diversity was not just about incidental customs but also about the way the gospel was expressed and the pattern of local church life. At the very heart of the apostolic mission there was a dynamic of diversity in relation to the one true gospel. Clearly there was no univocal language of the Christian gospel. In combination with this diversity there was also a commitment to extensive connections of fellowship with those in other places who belonged to the same Lord Jesus Christ.

We have seen how different local traditions grew up from these beginnings, and patterns of sustaining the wider fellowship of the whole Christian community emerged. We have also looked at three illustrative "moments" for Anglicans in different times and places. In England the 1662 Act of Uniformity suppressed the local diversity in favor of a more general uniformity, a model that yielded to stages of modification in the following three hundred years. In the U.S. the constitution established the new nation on the basis of inalienable individual rights. The Virginia Statute of 1785 removed religion from the public domain of politics in favor of a completely secular—that is, non-religious—conception. This model was adopted in the first amendment of the U.S. constitution and in the twentieth century extended to all states in the union. In the nineteenth century Australia retained the modified English pattern but moved it in a wider, deliberately plural direction and removed any establishment.

The faithfulness of Anglicans in engaging with their local circumstances has meant that not only has diversity emerged but the whole enterprise of understanding the assumptions and thinking implicit in those local circumstances has become very difficult for those located in other places.

The history of Christianity and of the Anglican tradition has also shown up differences that have not grown out of this faithfulness but from quite different forces. The church has been called to repentance, penitence, and restitution in recent years for some of the moral practices of the church community. Similarly, differences of opinion on elements of the faith have invoked the notion of heresy. In both these areas, the Christian church, and Anglicans amongst them, have tried to develop ways of dealing with such unacceptable diversity through penitential and disciplinary procedures.

It has not always been clear where to draw the line on these matters or how firmly to draw that line. When Paul wrote to the Corinthians about the hairstyles of women and men and implications about how each should pray, his argument drew on what "nature itself" teaches about long and short hair for men and women. He concluded his set of arguments by declaring that "if anyone is disposed to be contentious—we have no such custom, nor do the churches of God" (1 Cor 11:16). In relation to a matter of gross immorality earlier in the letter, he told them to "drive the wicked person from among you" (1 Cor 5:13). When he enumerates the "works of the flesh" in Gal 5:16–21, he tells his readers that "those who do such things will not inherit the Kingdom of God." Some things have been clear, others not so.

As a consequence there has been an ongoing debate in the church about where to draw the line on some things. Changing circumstances create new questions. This is true when the church has encountered new cultural contexts where different assumptions apply. It is also true where changing cultural assumptions re-focus an issue so that what was once clear is now not so clear. In the major Christian traditions there are fairly clear frameworks for the main lines of such arguments. In Anglicanism these have been fairly clear in general terms, though not as precise as in some other Christian traditions such as the extensive canon law of the Roman Catholic Church.

These are not simply matters of rational understanding. They clearly involve reasoned argument and understanding, but there is more involved here. We can see the deeper issues at stake in Paul's letter to the Romans. His exposition of the full forgiveness of God in the first five chapters confronted him with the question of agency in Christian living. "Should we remain in sin in order that grace may abound?" (Rom 6:1). His answer to that question is clearly no, and the reason is that the Christian is someone who is bound to Christ and thus alienated from sin. On the basis of this intimate relationship with Christ, he says, "do not let sin exercise dominion in your mortal bodies, to make you obey their passions" (Rom 6:12). It is not surprising that he then goes on in chapter seven to talk about the power of sin and the power of the Spirit of God. The Christian is caught in a power struggle. The terms of that struggle go through various formulations in chapters seven and eight but the conclusion is clear. Christians are to live according to the Spirit and not the flesh and the power of sin that is implicit in that allegiance.

Throughout Paul's letters the Christian is portrayed as someone in whose life the Spirit of God is at work. The Christian thus caught up in this divine dynamic is also confronted with the power of sin. The struggle is not against flesh and blood but against principalities and powers. Paul uses this kind of language in Romans in a way that highlights the layers of meaning in his understanding of the social situation of his readers. First in Romans 13 he tells them to submit to the "powers that be." This refers to the officers of the Roman government. This is not really an argument for political activity. On the contrary, he warns his readers to pay all their dues and to owe no one anything, to remain separate. Keep clear of evil because the day of salvation is at hand. The Christians should avoid the works of darkness. The policy of submission was at root a policy for being a resident alien, for people whose citizenship is in heaven. It is an explication of his initial exhortation not "to be conformed to this world, but to be transformed by the renewing of your minds, so that you may discern what is the will of God—what is good and acceptable and perfect"

(Rom 12:2). This different theological orientation of the Christian meant that there was always the possibility, indeed the probability, that Christians would be in conflict with the powers in the social and political world in which they lived out the terms of the gospel.

But it is all very well for Paul to advise his readers not to be conformed to this world and to be transformed by the renewing of their minds. It is quite another matter to see how that non-conformity is to be effected and what it might look like in actual conduct. This is especially so when the gospel commitment of Christians is to live out the character of the gospel in the terms of the circumstances in which they find themselves. How do we discern when we are subject to such subtle and pervasive influences from the forces at work in our own societies? Such a picture of Christians is given by Diognetus in the second century: "they show forth the character of their own citizenship in a marvelous and admittedly paradoxical way by following local customs in what they wear and what they eat and in the rest of their lives."[1] How to work towards such a situation is not so straightforward, and behind many of the conflicts between Anglicans around the world today lie different ways of dealing with the powers.

In 1996 Rodney Stark published an extraordinarily popular and well-received book, *The Rise of Christianity: A Sociologist Reconsiders History.* His answer, after a study of various aspects of the social setting and practices of the early Christians is that these Christians lived and acted as Christians are supposed to live.

> Christianity revitalized life in Graeco-Roman cities by providing new norms and new kinds of social relationships able to cope with many urgent urban problems. To cities filled with the homeless and impoverished, Christianity offered charity as well as hope. To cities filled with newcomers and strangers, Christianity offered an immediate basis for attachments. To cities filled with orphans and widows, Christianity provided a new and expanded sense of family. To cities torn by violent ethnic strife, Christianity offered a new basis for social solidarity. And to cities faced with epidemics, fires, and earthquakes, Christianity offered effective nursing services.[2]

Rodney Stark's work gives flesh to the claim of Tertullian, "It is our care of the helpless, our practice of loving kindness that brands us in the eyes

1. Ehrman, *Apostolic Fathers*, 2:140f.
2. Stark, *Rise of Christianity*, 161.

of many of our opponents. 'Only look,' they say, 'look how they love one another.'"[3]

These Christians did not by any means have it all their own way. The religious commitments of the government powers brought upon them waves of persecution and suffering. That did not provoke from the Christians rebellion, or revolution. Rather this hostility sharpened their social commitment and transformative living faith.

Four years later Stark, together with Roger Finke, addressed the modern situation of Christianity and of religion generally in a work that sought to bring to public attention a revolution in the way in which the sociology of religion was construed. They set out to shift what they called the old paradigm and in the process set out to bury the secularization theories of the founding fathers of sociology. They drew attention to the coincidence of the rise and public currency of atheism with the establishment of the old paradigm and highlighted assumptions in that paradigm; religion is false and harmful, religion is doomed (what came to be known as the secularization thesis), and religion is an epiphenomenon—that is to say, it had no claim to any kind of reality. The founders of the discipline and creators of this earlier paradigm rarely examined religion as a social phenomenon and were in fact primarily interested in highlighting "the harmful effects of religious pluralism and to stress the superiority of monopoly faiths."[4]

The new paradigm described by Stark and Finke rejects almost all of these elements. It affirms that religious choices and commitments are made on the basis of a more subjective and, for them, a more realistic version of rationality. The result of this reconfiguration is that religion is best thought of as operating in a kind of religious economy. This model is taken straight from the discipline of economics and even acknowledges a passing reference to public choice theory:

> We use the term "economy" in order to clarify that, in terms of certain key elements, the religious subsystem of any society is entirely parallel to the subsystem involved with the secular (or commercial) economy: both involve the interplay of supply and demand for valued products. Religious economies consist of a market of current and potential followers (demand), a set of organizations (suppli-

3. Tertullian, *Apology*, chapter 39; quoted by Stark, *Rise of Christianity*, 87.
4. Stark and Finke, *Acts of Faith*, 31.

ers) seeking to serve that market, and the religious doctrines and practices (products) offered by the various organizations.[5]

These two books show the situation at two different levels. The second is at a greater level of generality; how Christianity appears within the plurality of religions in society. The analysis tries not to discriminate between the truth claims of the individual religions, indeed it does not consider them at all except to say that they can be understood within an acceptable conception of human knowledge. In this respect the picture is different from the older approach to the sociology of religion, which carried with it anti-religion assumptions. The difficulty is that some religions claim a more public character than just plausibility. Some, Christianity amongst them, claim that the God to which they testify is truly the God of the universe and not simply, in Roman terms, a *superstitio*. So the critical question becomes, How far are the assumptions tacit in the social life of a community sympathetic to or committed to such a particular understanding? Does the society as a general rule assume for its operation that a particular religion is in some public sense true? That was the focus of the first book on the early Christians.

That world of contested realities is vividly set forward in the account of the martyrdom of Polycarp, Bishop of Smyrna, who was killed in the arena in Smyrna. The story is clearly written with the story of Jesus' crucifixion in mind. There is an interrogation with the Proconsul who tried to persuade him to swear by the genius of Caesar and to revile Christ. With miraculous coloring, the account describes in detail how Polycarp remained faithful and died a martyr.

Lest it be lost in terms of time and place, the document gives the characteristic dating details for both Romans and Jews, but then adds the Christian reality that had been manifested in the testimony of Polycarp:

> But the blessed Polycarp bore his witness unto death on the second day of the new month of Xanthikos, February 23, on a great Sabbath, at 2:00 in the afternoon. But he was arrested by Herod while Philip of Tralles was high priest, Statius Quadratus was proconsul, and Jesus Christ was ruling as king forever. To him be the glory, honour, greatness, and eternal throne, from one generation to the next. Amen.[6]

5. Ibid., 35f.

6. Ehrman, *Apostolic Fathers*, 1:397.

The reality of the Roman world indicated by their calendar is eclipsed by the reality of Jesus Christ reigning forever. Similarly, even the Jewish calendar is overcome by Jesus, the cosmic Lord of time. Here indeed is a contested reality in the denotation of time and the calendar. This is not religious products for private consumption. It is recognition of the result of the conflict between these great public realities.

What makes the contest so clear is that, as a good Roman, the Proconsul does not think that offering a libation to the Emperor is of much personal religious moment; it was simply a religious way of expressing political loyalty to the Emperor. He interprets allegiance to Christ in a similar way when he tells Polycarp to revile the Christ. This is politics in religious language. However what lies behind that belief is a particular conception of religious activity that Polycarp and the Christians could not share. For the Proconsul, personal religion was a matter of private opinion and practice—it was a *superstitio*.[7] Perhaps one might even say it was religious products for private consumption. Public religion was a more formal matter and had to do with civic loyalty and belonging. Polycarp could not make that separation. For him, and for the Christians, the Lordship of their crucified God was exclusive and reached to every aspect of their lives, personal, private, and public. Thus, to express political loyalty in pagan religious terms was not possible for them.

In just the same way the Christians could not deny Christ, even when that was in a context where the issue was clearly political. Polycarp tells the Proconsul that he would willingly converse with him about the Christian truth, for "we have been taught to render honour, as is meet, if it hurts us not, to princes and authorities appointed by God."[8] The claim of Christian writers in this period, and also later, was that they were loyal citizens and honored the Emperor, but they were not able to express that loyalty in religious terms because of their commitment to the Christ as universal Lord, and for the same reason they were not able to deny the connection of Christ's lordship with any aspect of life, including political life. Had the test of political loyalty been cast in non-religious terms, perhaps in moral or legal terms, then the conflict may not have arisen.

This situation for Christians has persisted throughout history, albeit in quite different formulations. On the January 26, 1788, Governor Arthur

7. See Lane Fox, *Pagans and Christians*; and MacMullen, *Paganism in the Roman Empire*.

8. Martyrdom of Polycarp X, Ehrman, *Apostolic Fathers*, 1:381.

Philip took possession of what was then called New South Wales, to establish a new British penal colony. Just three years after the passing of the Virginia Statute, Governor Philip took the usual oaths and declarations on February 10, 1788, in front of the assembled convicts and soldiers on the uncultivated soil of Port Jackson. The first two oaths concerned overt political authority and loyalty and then he declared:

> I, Arthur Phillip, do declare That I do believe that there is not any transubstantiation in the Sacrament of the Lord's Supper or in the Elements of Bread and Wine at or after the Consecration thereof by any Person whatsoever.[9]

Whether or not this represented Philip's personal religious views is hard to tell. But he understood clearly that the issue here was not his personal religious views, but loyalty to the English crown that was wedded to the Church of England as the religion of the nation. In 1788 Roman Catholicism was seen as politically subversive and so political opposition to it was officially focused on what was seen as the central defining tenet, the doctrine of transubstantiation.

That political hegemony of Anglicanism has now disappeared from the face of the earth. Anglicans today face the challenge of relating to the powers and forces at work in very different social and political circumstances. This is true of every province in the Anglican Communion. The tribal ethnic backgrounds of the people of Africa are not the same as those artificial lines drawn at the Berlin Africa Conference in 1884, and which created the shape of the current nation states of Africa. These ethnic tribal traditions are often mixed in the national Anglican churches and complicate the nature of the community of Anglicans in those provinces that correspond in large measure to the old colonial areas. It is hard even to speak of an African approach except in a very general way.[10] In the so-called Western countries in the Anglican Communion, there is a great deal of plurality in large part created by modern immigration and the plurality encouraged by national constitutions. These national categories are very general and do not always assist understanding.

It is sometimes thought that fellowship or communion is dependent on mutual understanding and agreement and that therefore the first chal-

9. Watson and Chapman, *Historical Records of Australia*, 1:21.

10. See, for example, Parratt, *Reinventing Christianity*; and Parratt, *Reader in African Christian Theology*.

lenge for Anglicans worldwide is to achieve better understanding. There is a certain truth in this but not nearly enough truth. Fellowship or communion depends as much on trust in the face of difference. Anglicans whom I do not fully understand cannot be cast beyond the pale of my Christian affection and fellowship. Even those whom I do understand to some extent and with whom I disagree on some issues are not thereby excluded from my fellowship.

Nonetheless mutual understanding within the church is not something to be put aside. Rather developing such mutual understanding is a challenge to be embraced. After all, the gospel did not begin with us, just as Paul reminded the Corinthians that it did not begin with them. Paul had to point out to the Corinthians that such an attitude inevitably had as its partner a form of arrogance that corrupts faith and behavior.[11] In order to underline how apparently similar parts of the Anglican Communion have underlying differences, I wish to return to the examples of Australia and the U.S. to which I referred in the previous chapter. I pointed out there in relation to the constitution and the Virginia Statute that the U.S. is built on a basis of inalienable individual rights and that the right to religious freedom came in that statute by the removal of religion from the public sphere. The foundational image of a wall of separation, first invoked by Roger Williams in the seventeenth century, created an environment where those opposed to religion could argue that it had no place in civic virtue—that, in Richard Rorty's phrase, democracy came before philosophy. It also created a situation where the personal conscience of the citizen was protected from the intrusive power of the state so long as that conscience was kept private.

The history of the U.S., however, has shown that religion has been a very present voice in public life. How are we to explain this apparent contradiction? The point has been well addressed on a number of occasions by Stephen Carter, who is professor of Law at Yale University. His bestselling book, *The Culture of Disbelief*, argued that the demand that religion have no place in public debate trivialized religion and forced the religious believer—and Carter had in mind especially the Christian—to deny her faith if she were to enter public life and debates. How could it be that a Christian should be expected to speak on such important things as justice and the care of the poor or weak in society without reference to

11. See 1 Corinthians 4.

the foundations of her views in Christian faith? Such a demand not only trivialized religious devotion, it created a culture of disbelief. In a second book on this theme, Carter turned to the constitution and the treatment of dissent. Here he focused on what he saw as government pressure to conform that was increasingly exerted on Christian believers. Carter argued that the constitution protected the liberty of the citizen to dissent. Harsh treatment of dissent by the government undermined both the liberties enshrined in the constitution and also the integrity of the government.[12]

However his most extensive and developed treatment of the theme of religion and politics in America came in his 2000 book *God's Name in Vain*. Here he argued two major theses. First, that there is nothing wrong, and much right, with the robust participation of the nation's many religious voices in debates over matters of public moment. Second, that religions—although not democracy—will almost always lose their best and most spiritual selves when they choose to be involved in the partisan, electoral side of American politics.[13]

Carter documents the involvement of religious people and religious arguments in a number of key social debates. He draws attention to the fact that America is one of the most religious of the Western nations, a view shared by Philip Jenkins.[14] The open role of religion in public debate has been an honorable and important part of the American story in the modern world. Carter notes particularly the ecclesial basis of the language of the civil rights movement in the twentieth century.

Yet somehow there are dangers in the involvement of religions in the public debates. Carter draws attention to the famous occasion at the Presidential Prayer Breakfast in September 1998 when then-President Clinton went public on national television about his behavior towards Monica Lewinsky: "There is no clever way to say that I have sinned."[15] The president's supporters cheered, thus making it clear that this was not really a religious moment, but a political one. As Carter says:

> And there lies the difficulty when God-talk mixes with the partisan side of politics: More than likely, for too many people with causes to push and desires to fulfill, the name of God will collapse

12. Carter, *Dissent of the Governed.*
13. Carter, *God's Name in Vain*, 1.
14. See Jenkins, *Next Christendom.*
15. Carter, *God's Name in Vain*, 15.

into a mere rhetorical device. Instead of maintaining the sacred character guaranteed by the Third commandment, God's name becomes a tool, a trope, a ticket to get us where we want to go.[16]

Some, however, did not cheer President Clinton's confession. A number of religious leaders published an open letter in which they said that they feared "that announcing such meetings to convince the public of the President's sincerity compromises the integrity of religion."[17] For his own part, Carter thinks that religions that get too regularly involved in politics loose their capacity to "engage in witness from afar."[18] From the point of view of Christianity, this means that such bodies run the risk of loosing their sense of divine vocation. The strange and wonderful vocation to which Diognetus referred is corrupted and lost. The citizenship that is in heaven becomes the citizenship that is more located here on earth and in the seats of the powerful. The long flirtation of Anglicans with the state makes this a peculiarly pointed temptation for Anglicans.

The second point Carter makes is that those who become electorally involved with a particular party are inevitably caught up in the logic of doing whatever has to be done in order to win the election. In other words, the logic of that party engagement takes over from their more fundamental obligations as Christians. This might be the equivalent of the Church of England as the Tory Party at prayer, though it is well represented in the internal party politics of modern Anglicanism.

On a number of occasions Carter refers to the way in which the U.S. government can reward churches for their support and punish those whom they do not appreciate through the taxation system. He has in mind the government's power to decide which churches are granted tax-exempt status, and he illustrates the issue by referring to incidents involving Bob Jones University and Robert Fuller's church. With some irony, he declares, "It should at least occasion a bit of comment that the federal government decides which benefits to grant or to deny to religions depending on the content of their teaching."[19]

Clearly Carter directs his argument against the modern version of the powers that face Christians in America. He claims that it is an inver-

16. Ibid., 16.

17. Carter, *God's Name in Vain*, 17.

18. Ibid., 22.

19. Ibid., 69.

sion of the position of the framers of the constitution.[20] Those powers seek to keep Christian faith in a so-called private realm and require religion to stay out of the public sphere. Furthermore, even when religion has so clearly entered into the public arena, it has often been manipulated for political purposes. As a result, church entry into politics is a risky business and according to Carter should not be undertaken too often. When churches do get involved in politics, they should choose the issues very carefully.

While this argument is judicious and restrained itself, it is nonetheless set within a basic American understanding of the nature of the constitution and of civil society. Carter's emphasis falls on the rights of individuals to freedom of religion both in terms of private practice and also by participating in the general life of society. He claims that the religion clause in the First Amendment was designed to protect religion from state interference. While that was probably Roger William's intention, it does not seem to me to have been the conception of Jefferson nor of the secular solution to the issue of religious pluralism generally in the eighteenth century. That solution meant the government may not make laws to establish religion, and while individuals may campaign on public issues out of religious motivations, in the end the means of persuasion will be political. Carter amply demonstrates the limitations of religious argument in political decision-making. Religious appeals may persuade numbers of citizens to support a cause such as the abolition of slavery or civil rights for African Americans, but the achievements of those goals under the assumptions of this commonwealth are political.[21]

Carter's books certainly shows that religious arguments in civic life have a long and extensive history in the United States. If the intention of Jefferson and the promoters of the First Amendment has been to keep religion out of public debate, then clearly they have failed; though not entirely, for Carter's discussion shows also that political engagement by religious bodies does not alter the fact that in the end political decisions are political not religious.

20. Ibid., 72.

21. Carter draws attention to the fact that action by Roman Catholic bishops on social issues gained public liberal support not on the grounds that bishops should intervene in political affairs but because of the character of the causes on which they acted. See ibid., 109.

There is a further point that emerges from the work of Stephen Carter, though he does not specifically develop it. Whatever the constitution says, the citizens of the U.S. are very religious, and the great majority of them go to church. This social experience means that there is readily available to public figures in the U.S. a language of social life drawn from the Christian tradition. That language is the language of the politics of the church—that is to say, how the church understands itself and seeks to fulfill its vocation.

Given that there are so many in the population influenced by this language from their churchgoing, it is not surprising that politicians and public figures seeking to persuade a multitude to follow them use this language. In the process of transposing this religious language from the community of the church to the secular pragmatics of public life, the meaning of the language is changed. It loses its essential, community-defining context. The kingdom of God is turned into the American republic. Thus the very popularity of religion among the people means that the language of religion not only becomes part of the rhetoric of politics, but also that in the process it is corrupted. The numerical support for Christian faith lays the foundations for the public corruption of its language. Such a process might be thought of as the democratic form of the Constantinian bondage of the church.

For Anglicans in this society, the framework of assumptions and the realities of political life directly affect the way in which they engage with their society. How they formulate their response to matters like gender relationships inevitably arises in a context in which the Christian way to be resident aliens giving witness to the truth of the gospel is not always clear. That the Anglicans in America are divided on these issues ought not to be surprising. Nor should it be surprising to us that the way in which they are divided and the way in which they think about the issues is different from the approach of Anglicans in other contexts.

There are many parts of the Anglican Communion where the cultural and political assumptions are clearly very different from the U.S. It is not hard to imagine that Nigerians or Kenyans engage with their local contexts on different assumptions and terms from those in the U.S. There are manifest differences that lie on the surface and are readily seen. Desmond Tutu, who has traveled often between these two continents, explained it in a lecture in New York this way:

> Unlike Westerners, Africans have a synthesizing mind set, as opposed to the occidental analytical one. That doesn't mean Africans are better or worse; it just means that God is smart. Westerners have analysis. We have synthesis. Westerners have a very strong sense of individualism. We have a strong sense of community.[22]

He argued that this difference was one of the reasons why the Truth and Reconciliation Commission was possible at all. It was because it "was consistent with a central feature of the African *Weltanschauung*—what we know in our language as *ubuntu.* . . . We belong in a bundle of life. We say, 'A person is a person through other persons.' It is not 'I think therefore I am.' It says rather: 'I am human because I belong. I participate, I share.'"[23] This does not mean that there is no sense of community or connectedness in the West nor individuation in Africa. Rather Tutu's point is that connectedness in the human condition is approached from different starting points and as a result any particular issue in life may well be configured differently. Such underlying cultural habits of thought and approach inevitably make mutual understanding between differently located groups problematic.

Tutu draws attention to such differences where the cultural images and instruments are manifestly different. But such underlying differences can exist where the cultural artifacts look very similar. Australia looks very like the U.S. on the surface—partly because of close political ties over many years and also due to the effects of years of imported American popular culture. But, as we saw in the previous chapter, the underlying constitutional and political assumptions are quite different in these two countries.

Australians are often puzzled at the religious language of much public debate in the U.S., in what professes to be a secular state, and where there is said to be a "wall of separation" between church and state. On the other hand, in Australia, where there is no such wall of separation, and the constitutional position is quite different, religion hardly figures in public debate.[24] This pattern has been challenged in recent years during the time of the Howard government and the more overt importance of the American Alliance. Some Australian commentators see in this period

22. Desmond Tutu, "Where Is Now Thy God?" Address to Trinity Institute, 1989, Diocese of East Oregon; quoted here from Battle, *Reconciliation*, v.

23. Tutu, *No Future without Forgiveness*, 31.

24. See the complaints of some historians—for example, Shaw, "Judeo-Christianity."

the importation of an American "religious right," which is out of place in the Australian tradition. The debate is reflected in the book *God Under Howard: The Rise of the Religious Right in Australian Politics* by Marion Maddox. She puts the origins of the book in this way: "I became interested in the increasingly organized efforts of an American-style religious right to gain a foothold in Australia's historically more secular democratic institutions. *God Under Howard* develops that theme in new directions."[25] In the book, Maddox sets out a view of the political tactics of John Howard, who was Prime Minister of Australia from 1996–2007. It is not a particularly sympathetic account, but the episodes she describes provide an example of the way in which the relation between religion and public life is debated in Australia and the kinds of issues that an Anglican might encounter in that context.

In 1992 the Australian High Court in the Mabo decision recognized Native Title, a recognition that was given legislative expression by the Labor government of Paul Keating. When Howard came to power in 1996, he put forward a Ten Point Plan that would have modified aspects of the Native Title legislation and re-directed government policy in a more social-development direction. This Ten Point Plan drew forth the almost universal condemnation of church leaders and national church organizations.

Maddox's analysis of Howard's tactics in dealing with religious arguments about public policy begins with this episode. She identifies a number of tactics.

- Drive a wedge between church leaders and their congregations. One government parliamentarian, Warren Entsch, told parishioners to boycott churches if clergy would not consult the congregation and represent the views of the parishioners in what they said publicly. In the Anglican tradition there is a thousand-year history of such matters, and the independence of the clergy has been enshrined in canon law for as long.

- Cultivate "others with a more extreme view than your own, making yourself look moderate by comparison."[26] In regard to Warren Entsch's remarks Howard simply said that he understood Mr

25. Maddox, *God under Howard*, xi.
26. Ibid., 145.

Entsch's frustration. "I do not support a call for a boycott of church attendance, but I can understand the sense of frustration he feels."[27]

- Set out rules by which church leaders should participate in public debate. Be informed, objective, and constructive. Submit to criticism from others. Do not allow the impression that clergy speak for all the members of their church.

- Brand opponents as extreme, thus putting your own position at the moderate centre.

- Point out divergences of opinion within the churches. Divide and conquer. Maddox quotes Howard as follows: "you can't assume that, for example, Archbishop Carnley speaks for the entire Anglican Church, he speaks essentially for himself and some body of opinion within the Anglican Church. . . . At the end of the day nobody owns the moral conscience of the nation. At the end of the day we all make our own moral judgments, they (the clergy) don't have superior ownership of moral issues."[28]

- Accuse "the churches of abandoning their proper role to become merely 'partisan.'"[29]

- Churches should stick to "spiritual leadership."

- In the course of this account Maddox claims there was a growing connection with Pentecostal churches who were generally regarded as right wing politically and sympathetic to Howard.

It seems to me that there is nothing special about these tactics. They are the common tools of daily political life. They do not show that Howard is manipulating religion or religious issues in some new and underhand way. Rather they show that Howard is a standard-run politician, intent on wining the argument, and that in turn simply reveals the will-to-power that marks aspects of politics in any society. It is not unlike Stephen Carter's reference to party politics being strictly about winning power.

At the end of her analysis, Maddox claims that Howard "has not entirely had his way with Australia's soul."[30] She offers as evidence for this

27. Ibid., 146.
28. Ibid., 148f.
29. Ibid., 149.
30. Maddox, *God Under Howard*, 319

that there were large demonstrations for "reconciliation" between indigenous Australians and others, that there was a letter writing campaign against the government's refugee internment policy, and that there were large public demonstrations against the Iraq war. The soul she has in mind is "Australia's democratic, egalitarian soul."[31] That is to say, its political soul, not its religious soul.

Her analysis shows something else, albeit indirectly. It shows that the language of the churches in these debates is the language that Howard insisted upon. It was political language. Church attendance is not as high in Australia as in the U.S. The use of religious language in politics does not yield as much rhetorical clout as it does in the U.S. Furthermore, the language used in Australian public life, as seen in this analysis, and in the wider literature on Australian social life, shows that secular language has carried the rhetorical day in politics in a way that is significantly less true in the U.S. In the U.S., the very success of the Christian churches provided the basis for the adoption of their language in politics, and in due course the colonization and corruption of that language.

In Australia there is a further complication in the interface between church and society because of the changed social position of the two major Christian traditions, the Anglicans and the Roman Catholics. Historically, the Anglicans have been the largest and the most influential church and Roman Catholics have been a significant minority. In the nineteenth century the Roman Catholics developed a social tradition of minority dissenters. They opted out of the public school system and established their own social institutions. Suddenly in the second half of the twentieth century they found themselves to be the largest church in the country and to have succeeded in producing through their educational system a wave of intellectuals, creative artists, and professionals that gave them an informal religious hegemony. The transition from minority dissenter to majority leader has not been easy for Roman Catholics in Australia. In the same period the Anglicans, on the other hand, had assumed too much of their establishment position from the colonial period and did not develop any significant intellectual tradition of social teaching. In the late twentieth century they have found themselves relegated to the role of a minority without the language or intellectual tools to deal with their

31. Maddox, *God under Howard*, 319.

situation. Both traditions flounder at the beginning of the twenty-first century, but for different reasons.

Anglicans thus find themselves in quite different situations in these apparently similar countries. In the U.S., there is a well-established and very American Anglican intellectual tradition. American Anglicans have not only engaged with their culture over a long period of time, they have been influenced by it. They have had their own period of empire and contain within their constitution overseas dioceses that are deemed to be part of The Episcopal Church of the United States of America as Province IX. They approach social issues within the framework of the constitutional foundations of their country and culture and its republican and individual rights culture. The public language of faith for American Anglicans has been in no small measure colonized by the secular. This colonization has made all the more complicated, and distinctly ambiguous, the vital question of responding to the powers at work in the social world in which they are called to witness to the transcendent Lord Jesus. Overlaid with this is the particular burden of being part of a world power in the mature phase of its imperial cycle. For Anglicans who are redeemed by a crucified savior, this is especially acute, as English Anglicans found in the nineteenth century.

In Australia, the situation is quite different. Anglicans operate within a framework that is more foundationally communitarian than is the U.S. They also operate in a situation where Christian affiliation is declining and where the history of the twentieth century has produced a public debate about the nature of society and its institutions that have become more overtly secular. Combined with the demise of an Anglican hegemony, and the consequent confusion about the language of faith in the public sphere, Anglicans are laid open to the colonization of the language of their faith generally and thus of being secularized. One can see this in the attempt to make the church a provider of a particular brand of otherwise undifferentiated spirituality in a market that seeks to satisfy the hunger left by materialism.

The point of these two examples is that, despite the appearance of considerable similarity between Australia and the U.S., the underlying cultural assumptions and forces are in fact quite different. That means that the encounter with the powers, the challenge not to be conformed to this world but to be transformed in our minds, is set in quite different circumstances and thus naturally produces quite different responses to social issues as they arise. If there are such differences between these two closely related countries, how much greater will be the challenges of mutual understanding where the differences are much greater and more obvious?

Because Anglicans have historically been committed to the local, and to witness in the terms of the local, these differences flourish and develop. The challenge therefore in an international fellowship of churches comes to its sharpest point in the faithful engagement of Anglicans with their local situations and the powers that operate in them. It is as we seek to pursue our "strange and wonderful" vocation that we inevitably and properly move in different directions. The appropriate theological question therefore is not, how can we agree on common policies and practices on social matters? Nor is the question, how can we enforce some kind of uniformity? The experience of our English Anglican friends has shown us that such an ambition is a snare. The real question is the one posed by Jesus. "By this shall all know that you are my disciples, if you love one another"[32] and repeated in a different form by Tertullian, "See, they say, how they love one another."[33]

32. John 13:35.

33. Tertullian, *Apology*, chapter 39, quoted from Roberts and Donaldson, *Ante-Nicene Fathers*.

# PART TWO

# Will the Current Anglican Experiment Go Anywhere?

# Introduction

Anglicans around the world are living out an experiment in how to connect differences in a universal and personal faith. Differences have arisen in the second half of the twentieth century over relations between men and women in the public life of the church. There had been earlier serious debate about the role of women in the governance structures of the church as church wardens and members of synods. The General Convention of ECUSA voted only in 1970 to admit women as lay deputies in the General Convention. The ordination of women was treated much more seriously. The first ordination had taken place in Hong Kong in 1945. This wartime initiative was not widely welcomed. However ordinations of women as priests began in 1974 in the U.S. with the irregular ordination in Pennsylvania of twelve women by a retired bishop. These ordinations were later regularized by resolution of the General Convention, and the first woman ordained as a bishop was Barbara Harris in 1989. There are now women priests and bishops in a number of provinces. These moves caused considerable conflict and have left some serious divisions among Anglicans around the world. However, much more serious conflict has emerged over the place of homosexuals in the public life of the church. The initial moves came in North America, and the conflict continues.

Like the Orthodox, Copts, Lutherans, and most other Christian traditions that have spread around the world, Anglicans have a loose global structure. The obvious single exception to this is the Roman Catholic Church. Anglicans first appointed an executive officer in 1959, and a representative body with a constitution approved by all the provinces in 1968. This loose structure reflects a long tradition of an ecclesiology that began at the local level and in institutional terms extended only to the province that contained a number of dioceses with a general synod and a metropolitan, usually called an archbishop. In some nations, provinces have joined together to form a national constitution, and sometimes provinces are co-extensive with a nation or include a number of nations.

The conflict over homosexuality in the public life of the church has been manifest within provinces and also between provinces. There are well-established institutions to deal with conflict within provinces, but not so at the global level. Anglicans have thus been coping with this conflict with new and slight global institutional arrangements. They have come to this conflict with little ecclesiological rationale for any global institutionality, indeed a reasonably long standing presupposition against any supra-provincial judicature. Several things have thus come together at the same time. Disagreement between provinces over homosexuality in the public life of the church has created inter-provincial conflict. Extra-provincial institutions are being created to contain this conflict. The new arrangements are to have some coercive powers over provinces. The resources in the Anglican theological tradition for such arrangements are meagre in the extreme. As a consequence this development is a very adventurous experiment in ecclesiology and very high risk in terms of *real-politic*. Anglicans thus provide an acted-out example of the challenge of connecting in the midst of conflict posed for a Christian tradition which is personal and thus local in its demands and also universal in its appeal and mission.

Part II looks at the progress of this experiment in the light of the analysis offered in Part I. The Anglican Communion and its embryonic structures have responded in stages to this challenge, represented first by the Virginia report and The Windsor Report which in turn has led to the so called "Windsor Process."[1] The conflict has not abated, and the outcomes of this ecclesiological experiment have not become clear. Even so, the staging posts along the way provide the points of reference for what follows. In using these points of reference, it should not be imagined that the Windsor Process is the only game in town. There are clearly other processes going on, and these make contact with the Windsor Process from time to time.

---

1. In the arguments that follow I have used and modified some of the material previously published in Kaye, "Unity in the Anglican Communion," and Kaye, "Power, Order and Plurality."

# 5

# Why the "Virginia Report" is Not Good Enough

THE "VIRGINIA REPORT" TAKES its name from the Virginia Theological Seminary, where the Inter-Anglican Theological and Doctrinal Commission held its meetings in December 1994 and again in January 1996[1] and produced their report. The 1988 Lambeth Conference responded to consultation from The Episcopal Church of the United States of America (ECUSA) about the possibility of a woman being consecrated as a bishop in ECUSA. A commission on women in the episcopate was established to examine the relationship between the provinces and to encourage and monitor consultation on the issue. This commission, chaired by Robin Eames, produced four brief reports, which when published together in 1994 became known as the Eames Report. It placed on the table the concept of *koinonia* as a way of understanding the unity of the Anglican Communion. The Lambeth Conference had called for "further exploration of the meaning and nature of communion with particular reference to the doctrine of the Trinity, the unity and order of the Church, and the unity and community of humanity."[2] After a preliminary consultation in 1991 the Inter-Anglican Theological and Doctrinal Commission was established to consider the responses to this consultation when it met in 1994 and 1996. Robin Eames also chaired this commission. The report was considered at the 1998 Lambeth Conference, but that conference was taken up with issues of sexuality. The debate the following year at the Anglican Consultative Council in Dundee, Scotland, was relatively con-

1. The text is published in the official reports of ACC X and the Lambeth Conference and is available online: http://www.aco.org/documents/virginia/english/index.html.

2. LC 1988 Resolution 18.

tentious, and the resolutions seem to reflect some caution about aspects of the report.[3]

The report sets out the question it was to address in terms of the unity of the Anglican Communion and how the highest degree of communion could be maintained. It relates its concerns with the exercise of authority in the communion and connects this with a request from the Lambeth Conference to The Anglican Roman Catholic International Commission to explore the possibility of a universal primacy.

The report follows closely the terms of its brief. It contains six chapters, the first of which sets out the broader cultural context of modern pluralism. This context frames the concerns of the report and is the impulse against which the report directs it attention. The report develops a theological approach to the question of independence and unity by looking first at the issue of communion and the doctrine of the Trinity applied to the church generally (chapter 2); belonging together in the Anglican Communion (chapter 3); levels of communion and the principle of subsidiarity and interdependence (chapter 4). Chapter 5 returns to the purpose and principles of *koinonia*. The final chapter is concerned with what are called "instruments of unity." This phrase was first developed in a small group chaired by Robin Eames that produced a memo for the 1988 Lambeth Conference that in turn shaped the key resolutions at that conference on the ordination of women. The language has come to describe the role of the Archbishop of Canterbury, the Lambeth Conference, the Anglican Consultative Council, and the Primates' meeting. These four so-called instruments of unity are the focus of the last chapter of the Virginia Report, and a series of questions is posed in this final chapter in relation to each of these "instruments." In 2005 the ACC changed the designation of the Archbishop of Canterbury to "Focus of Unity."

## Themes and Logic of the Argument

There are a number of themes that recur in this report and some of them are the subjects of specific exposition. These themes provide the theological and philosophical substructure upon which the argument of the report is developed.

---

3. See the analysis and description of the ACC XI debate in I. T. Douglas, "Authority After Colonialism."

## The Doctrine of the Trinity

The report reflects recent interest in Western theology in the doctrine of the Trinity in terms of the community that exists between the three persons of the Godhead. In the history of Christian theology, a distinction has often been made between the Trinity of the economy of salvation and the Trinity considered in terms of its inner being. It is commonly said that the Greek fathers in the early church came at this question from the perspective of economy of salvation and thus, in the terms of Karl Rahner, "the Greek way of thinking of the Trinity remains entirely orientated to man."[4] The Western tradition of thought, influenced in large measure by Augustine, moved away from this starting point and focused on the nature of the one Godhead. Miroslav Volf[5] compares the trinitarian formulation of Joseph Ratzinger, now Pope Benedict XVI, and the Orthodox theologian John Zizioulas. He argues that Ratzinger continues the Augustinian line and in the process underlines the unity of the Godhead with his emphasis on the Trinitarian personhoods as pure relationality—*persona est relatio.* Zizioulas, on the other hand, works within a Greek tradition and uses the model that underlines the inter-dependence of the *persona* and their reciprocal interiority, but within a non-filioquistic formulation. On this analysis, this model gives a priority to the Father and offers more prominence to hierarchy in the Godhead. This point becomes strategically important when we come to the question of the relation between Trinity and ecclesiology, an issue that is vital to the argument of the Virginia Report.

Miroslav Volf draws attention to this in his comparison of Ratzinger and Zizioulas. It lies not far below the surface in recent ecumenical dialogue documents, and in recent theological literature. Volf suggests that the unitary character of Ratzinger's formulation of the Trinity leads him to a unitary style of ecclesial relations, which enables him to place a universal primacy naturally in a logically prominent position. On the other hand, Zizioulas is enabled to give natural prominence to the priority of the bishop in a hierarchy in the light of the hierarchy of his Trinitarian formulation. Thus, in the former case, the separate identities of ecclesial communities are diminished, and in the latter case they are recognized within a hierarchical framework.

4. Karl Rahner, "Trinity in Theology."
5. Volf, *After Our Likeness.*

This simple contrast does not by any means exhaust the variations in the formulation of the doctrine of the Trinity available in the history of Christian theology. However, it does illustrate the point, which is not recognized in this report, that the formulation of the doctrine of the Trinity chosen will affect the way in which it is likely to work out when you come to the question of ecclesiology. Even if the matter is taken at the most general level, as this report tends to do, this issue cannot be avoided. This generality of treatment, however, gives the impression that the doctrine of the Trinity is being used in this report somewhat as a validating talisman.

However, the use of the doctrine of the Trinity in this report raises a further point, namely, the relationship between this use of the doctrine and the actual ecclesial reality out of which the argument is developed. Again Volf hints at this question, although his hint is buried in a footnote when discussing Zizioulas: "At least to me as an outsider, Zizioulas's unrestricted affirmation of hierarchy seems to correspond more to the Orthodox ecclesial reality than does the polemic against subordination in the church (directed especially against (Roman) Catholic ecclesiology) to which some Orthodox theologians are inclined."[6] One might, of course, also wonder whether Volf's own formulation of the doctrine of the Trinity echoes his own Free Church ecclesial reality.

I am not suggesting that people are not being transparent and that the Trinitarian argument is really a cloak for unstated ecclesiastical positions. Rather, my point is that these issues are interrelated, and the precise character of that interrelationship is not identified in the Report.[7] For example, the more unitary formulation of the doctrine of the Trinity in the hands of Ratzinger makes it easier to move to a conception of the church created by this Trinitarian God that should have one single point of reference for unity and authority, just as the insistence on the hierarchy of the Father in some orthodox formulations makes an ecclesiology marked by strong episcopal hierarchy more understandable. Such a tendency in the formulation of the Trinity could also in another context lead to an argument for a moral and divinely sanctioned hierarchy between men

6. Ibid., 215n103.

7. This is similar to Karl Barth's general point that church dogmatics arises in an ecclesial framework, and thus he came to write not Christian Dogmatics but Church Dogmatics. See *Church Dogmatics*, vol. 1, especially the personal preface of 1932 and pages 3–11.

and women.[8] These different emphases in the doctrine of the Trinity can drift into the outer limits of the dynamics of the doctrine and begin to approach the recognized heresies of the early church of subordinationism on the one hand and monarchianism on the other.

It should also be noted that the report does not address the question of whether the doctrine of the Trinity is an appropriate model for ecclesiology, or whether modeling is itself an appropriate approach to ecclesiology. It is true that the Lambeth Conference resolution setting out the terms of reference for the commission asked that the question should be pursued in relation to the doctrine of the Trinity. But that resolution was the work of a conference of over a thousand bishops who passed seventy-three resolutions that year. The commission contained expert theologians, and one might have expected a little more critical distance from the precise details of these terms of reference if they were at all doubtful about them. As it stands the report offers a very narrow approach to ecclesiology that closes down the conversation rather than opening it up.

## Communion (koinonia)

This theme has also been revived in Orthodox theology, particularly at the hands of John Zizioulas, again in relation to an ecclesiological question arising in modern Orthodoxy. The question in Orthodoxy is how to understand the relationship between the various Orthodox churches within the broader Orthodox family. Are these separate and autocephalous churches to be regarded as churches in their own right or as part of a greater church? Zizioulas's suggestion is that the greater church be thought of as a fellowship of churches and what holds them together is *koinonia*. Such a conception is more elastic and allows for a slightly larger arena of legitimate diversity. The Synod of Bishops of the Roman Catholic Church in 1985 declared in relation to Vatican II that "the ecclesiology of communion is the central and fundamental idea of the Council's document."[9] This was part of the underlying current in Vatican II to allow for more diversity and thus to broaden the base of coherence in the Roman Catholic

8. That argument is indeed made in a report of the diocese of Sydney in Australia so that women are barred from ordination as priests in the diocese and to holding a position as incumbent of a parish. This very interesting report is available at http://www.sds .asn.au/assets/documents/synod/TrinityDoctrineComm.pdf. It is critically discussed in Giles, *Trinity and Subordinationism*.

9. See "Church in the Word of God."

Church and enable more extensive local focus in ecclesiology. This aspect of Vatican II has not gained prominence in the life of the Roman Catholic Church since the council.

The idea has been taken up in ecumenical thinking in a somewhat different way. It is used to contain diversity rather than to ease conformity. Thus it was used to criticize divergent tendencies in the development of the individuality of churches and to argue for more connection. It became the centerpiece of the statement of the World Council of Churches (WCC) Assembly in Canberra in 1991[10] and has been used in a number of Anglican–Roman Catholic International Commission (ARCIC) documents.[11] In the Virginia Report, the notion of *koinonia* is used in much the same way as in these ecumenical dialogues. That is to say, it is used to enhance connection and coherence rather than to recognize diversity. In this respect, the report moves in a different direction from the report of the first IATDC, *For the Sake of the Kingdom.*[12]

Its application to the Anglican Communion in this report is interesting in another respect. It has long been held in major sections of Anglican thought that the Anglican Communion was not a church but rather a fellowship of churches. Arguments of this kind were used by some English bishops as the basis for not attending the first Lambeth Conference, and it has been the terms in which the Lambeth Conference has consistently described the Anglican Communion.[13] The Virginia Report does not manifest an awareness of this older and more consistent view of the Anglican

10. The document produced by the Canberra assembly can be found in the official report Kinnamon, *Signs of the Spirit.*

11. See the ARCIC final report: "This theme of koinonia runs through our statements" (Hill and Yarnold, *Anglicans and Roman Catholics*, 6).

12. ACC and IATDC, *For the Sake of the Kingdom.*

13. For example Lambeth Conference, 1930, Resolution 49 states, "The Anglican Communion is a fellowship, within the one Holy Catholic and Apostolic Church, of those duly constituted dioceses, provinces or regional Churches in communion with the See of Canterbury, which have the following characteristics in common:
   a. they uphold and propagate the Catholic and Apostolic faith and order as they are generally set forth in the Book of Common Prayer as authorised in their several Churches;
   b. they are particular or national Churches, and, as such, promote within each of their territories a national expression of Christian faith, life and worship; and
   c. they are bound together not by a central legislative and executive authority, but by mutual loyalty sustained through the common counsel of the bishops in conference."

Communion. That is perhaps not surprising given that the centralizing drive in the report undermines the older conception, but alas does so without engaging with it.

## Subsidiarity

In modern theology the principle of subsidiarity has been most widely used in the lead-up to Vatican II. The principle is that things should not be done at one level of decision-making that can be adequately or properly done at a lower level. This principle has had a long history in Gallican theology, and its revival in the French *nouvelle theologie* which was influential in the lead-up to Vatican II. This principle has been widely used by Roman Catholic theologians in order to critique an over-centralized hierarchical conception of the Papacy and the Vatican and church structure generally. In the hands of some Roman Catholic theologians, it has been part of an argument that contrasts a hierarchical and democratic church.[14]

Here in the Virginia Report, the concept is used to acknowledge the present structures but is not given the same force in the argument as the earlier conceptions of *koinonia* and Trinity. Given its intellectual pedigree, that is not surprising, since it would run against the centralizing and hierarchical current of the argument in this report.

## Episcope—Oversight

This report is strong in underlining the personal character of episcope. In this respect the report draws on a long tradition of Anglican apologetics directed towards Presbyterian and later dissenting movements. However, the report expands episcopacy so that the bishop has a complete oversight over all aspects of the life of the church. The bishop begins to look very much like a corporate Chief Executive Officer. There are some understandable difficulties in relation to this concept in a longer Anglican tradition rather than one that is envisaged as commencing with the sixteenth century as this report tends to assume. In the period up until the fifteenth century, the development of the character and pattern of episcopal responsibilities was gradual. It was often monastic in early periods; indeed monastic episcopacy was a distinctive mark of early Anglicanism.

14. See for example, Bianchi and Ruether, *Democratic Church*, and Hill, *Ministry and Authority*.

It is significant that the horizon of interpretation in the Virginia report is the English Reformation and its legislative form. In the English Reformation there was a significant revolution whereby bishops became crucial to the single jurisdictional authority of the Crown. One of the significant authority consequences of the abolition of the monasteries was that it narrowed institutional authority to the bishops, whose cathedrals, though very wealthy, were never abolished. That move had the effect of moving the diocesan bishops away from the older monastic model to being more a part of the institutional fabric of the state and royal rule. At the Hampton Court Conference in 1604, James I rejected prophesying on the grounds that it was a political threat to his crown saying,

> "that they aymed at a Scottish Presbytery, which, sayth he, as well agreeth with a monarchy, as God and the divell. Then Iack and Tom, and Will and Dick, shall meete, and at their pleasure censure me and my councill, and all our proceedings." And then turning to the bishops, the king said, "If once you were out, and they in place, I know what would become of my supremacie. No Bishop, no king."[15]

As far as James I was concerned, episcopacy as conceived under the statutes of the English Reformation was a model of authority not only compatible with, but supportive of the singular authority of the Royal Supremacy. In the period of colonial and imperial expansion, that model was extended beyond the borders of England, where eventually changes occurred that made it irrelevant and unworkable. The polity that appeared at the end was definitively synodical in character. The Virginia Report does not seem to have escaped from this sixteenth-century imperial or colonial framework.

## The English Reformation

Throughout this report respectful allusions are made to the English Reformation, but only a slender role is given to the Reformation, at least in terms of its theology. References sometimes appear to me to be out of focus. The reference at 4.21 to Hooker on consensus is an example, though later there is a correct note at 4.26 in regard to "Hooker and Field and

15. Barlowe, *Summe and Substance of the Conference*, 83, quoted in Jordan, *Development of Religious Toleration*, 19. For a critical appraisal of these events, see Curtis, "Hampton Court Conference and Its Aftermath."

ecclesiologies." The report also makes a good point at 3.3 that the Acts of Uniformity of the sixteenth century at least were attempts to contain diversity, though that certainly could not be said of the 1662 *Act of Uniformity*. Comment in 3.25 that in the sixteenth-century Reformation no attempt was made to minimize the role of bishops appears to me to be somewhat disingenuous since in institutional and legal terms the Reformation legislation actually increased the political and institutional significance of the bishops. The theological significance of the English Reformation is not systematically developed within the report, and its place in the longer run of Anglican Christianity is quite misleadingly portrayed.

## Primacy

While there are some modifiers in the report, the notion of primacy is shaped by the idea of primacy in the modern form of Roman Catholicism. But the modern form of the primacy in Roman Catholicism is the consequence of developments from the eleventh century in a very singular direction, developments accelerated during the course of the nineteenth century in response to the challenges of modernity. It represents a second millennium revolution in ecclesiology in the directions of clerical imperialism that Anglicans have fairly consistently rejected.[16] In 1930 the Lambeth conference addressed this issue, and the section report on the Anglican Communion put it in these direct and strong terms:

> There are two prevailing types of ecclesiastical organisation: that of centralised government, and that of regional autonomy within one fellowship. Of the former the Church of Rome is the great historical example. The latter type, which we share with the Orthodox Churches of the East and others, was that upon which the Church of the first centuries was developing until the claims of the Roman church and other tendencies confused the issue. The Provinces and Patriarchates of the first four centuries were bound together by no administrative bond: the real nexus was a common life resting upon a common faith, common Sacraments, and a common allegiance to an Unseen Head.[17]

This anti-imperialist sentiment in Anglicanism is persistent and reflects a long history in the tradition going back well before the sixteenth

16. See Kaye, *Introduction to World Anglicanism*.
17. *The Lambeth Conference, 1930*, 153.

century. Indeed, the final 1662 form of the English reformation was in this respect an exception to the longer history of Anglicanism rather than the norm.

There is an older model of the role of the metropolitan in the life of the church that is not developed in The Virginia Report and that was significant in the historical development of the Anglican Communion particularly in the nineteenth century. Once there were metropolitan bishops outside of England, in places where there was at least some degree of political independence, serious difficulties arose in regard to the politico–juridical conception of the metropolitical role of the Archbishop of Canterbury. In fact, it evaporated. The older notion of metropolitan understands the local province as ecclesially self-contained for jurisdictional purposes and for the purposes of completeness of order in the ministry. A more Anglican model of Primacy in Anglicanism is set within this older conception and more accurately reflects the strong provincial element in historical Anglican ecclesiology. By using the imagery of the Roman Catholic Church and its modern notion of Primacy, the report significantly misses crucial aspects of the broader history of early Christianity and of a more critical appreciation of the Anglican tradition of ecclesiology.

Moreover, the Anglican Communion should probably be regarded as being born in the concordat between the bishops of the Scottish Episcopal Church and Samuel Seabury over the significance of their consecration in 1784 of Seabury for The Episcopal Church in Connecticut.[18] The War of Independence broke the legal connection with England and thus with the legally established Church of England. The English bishops were prohibited from ordaining bishops for places outside of England. For this reason Seabury went to the Episcopal Church of Scotland seeking consecration. This episode is full of ironies. Seabury had supported the loyalist cause in the War of Independence, those who consecrated him were non-jurors, and back in the United States of America not all accepted Seabury, at least in part for his political commitments during the war. Even so, this step illustrated the fact that Anglican Christianity was transportable beyond England, a point made already by the existence of the Episcopal Church of Scotland. What was apparent in the Seabury consecration became again manifest in the growth of colonial churches as those colonies became

---

18. See Pritchard, *History of the Episcopal Church*, 88; and Thomas, "Unity and Concord."

independent, and where overseas provinces were established, such as in Australia in 1847. In these provinces, as in provinces in other parts of the world, the Archbishop of Canterbury had no metropolitical authority.

## Missing Links

A number of things are clearly missing in this report if it is to be considered a full and serious treatment of how Anglicans are to sustain appropriate relationships with each other.

### Congresses

Church congresses were a major force in holding sections of Anglicanism together regionally in the period 1860–1930. That was true in Australia, and it was true also in North America and England. That movement brought a cross-section of church people together on common concerns. There was a pan-Anglican congress in the first decade of the twentieth century motivated by similar intentions. The movement declined in influence in the early part of the twentieth century, perhaps in the face of sectional organizations and political events during the twentieth century that distracted attention and emboldened a more imperial notion of political leadership. Later in the century the principle was revived and Congresses were held in 1954 at Minneapolis and in 1963 in Toronto. An appendix to the Virginia Report comments in somewhat dismissive terms on a proposal to hold another congress.

The Meeting of the Anglican Consultative Council in Dundee, Scotland, in 1999 had welcomed a report for a Congress of the Anglican Communion and recommended that there should be such a Congress in association with the next Lambeth Conference and asked the Archbishop of Canterbury and the Secretary General to put in hand such planning and financial provision as would make this Congress a reality.

A Design Group prepared a report for the Archbishop of Canterbury and the Joint Standing Committee of the Primates with the intention that the ACC-12 in Hong Kong in September 2002 would take the Executive decision to proceed with the Gathering. The report underlined the value of a separate event residing in its capacity to stand as an alternative to activities that are sometimes marked by political tendencies and special interest interventions in a way that often eclipses the common grass-roots commitments and concerns of Anglican Christians around the world. The report articulated a vision for a Gathering that would:

1. gather Anglicans from every part of the Communion to celebrate the presence and activity of God in our lives *and in the world*;

2. call people to unite under the guidance of the Holy Spirit, sustained by Word, Sacrament, common prayer, and thanksgiving;

3. give people time and opportunity to know each other and to hear stories of Anglicans living in different cultures and traditions;

4. assist participants to confront those forces which diminish the quality and value of life;

5. empower Anglicans to renew their commitment to a clear Gospel mission and a vision of justice, peace, and fullness of life in Jesus Christ; and

6. return from the gathering inspired by a richer vision of the global Anglican community of faith and the challenge to engage with their own local community.

The program would have an over-arching mission theme and contain a good deal of storytelling, of worship and rejoicing in the grace of God, and in attending to the Scriptures in the form of Bible study. The program would encourage participants to dream dreams and be able to share them. There would be no resolutions, but everyone who participated in this Gathering would go home with a wider awareness of the activity of God in the lives of their fellow Christians in other parts of the world. They would therefore have a more vivid sense of their connectedness within the Body of Christ and of the commonalities that exist between themselves and other Anglicans around the world.

The Gathering was to be held in South Africa and would be preceded by a retreat for the Primates, with the Lambeth Conference following the Gathering at the same location. An organizing group was established and CPSA presented a final proposal to the 2005 meeting of the ACC.

This proposal was supported in principle by a variety of groups including the Primates' meeting and the Joint Standing Committee, previous meetings of the ACC and the Lambeth Conference, but in 2005 it was dropped at the meeting of the ACC presumably on funding grounds, though the records of the meeting give no clear reason for the decision.

The ACC at this meeting did ask its Standing Committee to consider the matter further, though nothing has since been heard on this subject. In the light of events since that decision, the 2008 Lambeth Conference has become a point of great political contention. A gathering would have been a great benefit in the developing hostilities in the communion. It must be one of the great lost opportunities of this generation of Anglicans.

## Regionalism

There are a variety of regional alliances and coalitions between provinces or parts of the Anglican Communion that are not mentioned in the Virginia Report and apparently not considered. Province 9 of ECUSA is a good example of the reach of that Church generally into Latin America and the Pacific. This is to say nothing of its reach into Europe, although there, of course, it overlaps with the reach of the Church of England. There is a multitude of informal connections of various kinds regionally that serve to hold different areas of the Anglican Communion in connection with each other. The Council of the Churches of East Asia, previously concerned with extra provincial dioceses in Asia but since the formation of the Province of South East Asia it continues as a regional liaison group. Council for the Anglican Provinces of Africa and the South Pacific Anglican Council are others.

## Networks Related to the Anglican Consultative Council (ACC)

For some time there has been a range of networks on various topics that are informal, mostly unfunded from the ACC budget, which nonetheless have had the recognition of the ACC and have brought people into coalitions of interest from the provinces around the Communion. The connections from various provinces to the office of the United Nations observer might be an example of such a network. Others are the Network for Inter-Faith Concerns in the Anglican Communion, International Family Network, The Anglican Indigenous Network, Anglican Peace and Justice Network, The Anglican Communion International Refugee and Migrant Network, International Anglican Women's Network, and the International Anglican Youth Network.

## Other Network Connections

There are a range of institutional connections that could be loosely called networks, which contribute to the tentacles of attachment between provinces in the Communion. The influence of Trinity Wall Street, though principally financial and grant-making in one sense, nonetheless provides a network of connection. The same is true of the Primate's World Development Fund within the Canadian church. There are a range of educational connections through scholarships and training and publishing. There are partnership connections, both formal and informal, through dioceses and provinces across the Communion. Furthermore, there is the global reach of the Mothers' Union, less noticed than some other things but significantly more important than some of the things mentioned in the Virginia Report.

Then there are the mission agencies and their continuing networks. In the nineteenth century these were powerful networks and the influence of the secretary of the Society for the Propagation of the Gospel (SPG) or Church Missionary Society (CMS) was often much more significant than that of the local bishop for any missionary working in a colonial diocese.[19]

Religious orders span the Communion, cross the provinces and provide connections of some considerable significance. Meetings of the provincial secretaries, though informal, nonetheless also contribute, in the words of Michael Peers, formerly the Primate of Canada, as the "glue of the Communion."[20]

It may be possible to draw some kind of distinction between these missing links and the four vehicles that are the focus of the Virginia Report but such a distinction is not attempted in the Virginia Report. Even if such a distinction were able to be made, a consideration of a smaller number of vehicles as in the Virginia Report, without seriously taking account of the context of other vehicles by which the Anglican Communion is held together, must lead to a significant distortion of the picture. In the case of this report, it certainly does.

19. See Cnattingius, *Bishops and Societies*.

20. The phrase was used by Peers at a meeting of provincial secretaries, at which the author was present, in September of 2000.

## The Historical and Theological Picture of Anglicanism

The Virginia Report appears to assume, but does not argue, that Anglicanism is a post-sixteenth-century phenomenon. Prior to that, it seems to be the view of the report that Anglicanism was simply part of Western Christianity. There are some gestures in the report towards the conciliar movement but not a lot of discussion about the pre-sixteenth-century elements of Anglicanism. As a consequence, the models that are used tend to be taken from the nineteenth and twentieth century. This is particularly true in my view in regard to episcopacy, primacy, ministry, and those matters to which the report gives logical priority in the life of the church, namely its ordered, mainly clerical structures rather than, for example, its local and dispersed life. This is a church that appears not to have any laity.

It is important to recognize that Anglicanism is part of Western Christianity with its own regional characteristics and with a much longer history than simply the last four hundred years. In some respects it is similar to the tradition within Western Christianity of Gallicanism. Gallicanism has had an intermittent history as a style of Western Christianity that has shown a degree of independence, local color, and commitment to the spiritual conception of the life of the church. In one sense the difference between Gallicanism and Anglicanism is that Gallicanism stayed within the Roman framework for political reasons and Anglicanism did not.[21] The movements towards centralism in the papalist/conciliar conflict in the fifteenth century led to the demise of Gallicanism, or at least its significant suppression under a centralizing papalistic conception of the Roman communion. Anglicanism in its conciliar form is a more complicated matter. The very legislation that supervened on the Church of England provided the possibility for sustaining conciliar elements of both theology and ecclesial thought within the life of the "empire of England" through the strained mechanism of the Royal Supremacy that established a layman as head of the church.[22]

In the English Reformation there was a religious revival that was part of the movement in Western Christianity of renewal that saw its expression in the Continental Reformation, as well as other earlier movements in Eastern and Central Europe. At the same time, there was a legislative,

21. See Avis, *Beyond the Reformation?*

22. See Cross, *Church and People*, which sets the matter in a broader historical context.

state-initiated revolution effected in order to secure political independence for the ecclesiastical laws that Henry wanted to be able to command. The sixteenth-century Reformation is, therefore, a coalescence of religious revival out of a long northern tradition of Christianity and social thought occurring hand-in-hand with a political revolution. Because the Virginia Report seems not to be able to see past the sixteenth century, the images it uses for its ecclesiological conceptions are drawn from the modern period both of Roman Catholicism and of English Christianity, which, each in different ways, significantly distort the longer tradition of British Christianity and thus of Anglicanism.

As a consequence the report in this respect is insufficiently rigorous in its conception of Anglicanism and, to that extent, is seriously misleading about its character and limited in its interpretation of that character.

## The Presenting Context

The presenting context offered by the report is that of pluralism and postmodern dispersion (chapter 1). If we assume such a characterization is fair, the question still remains as to what kind of response one might imagine to be appropriate for something like the Anglican Communion. Historically, times of uncertainty and flux, such as that portrayed in the postmodern interpretation of our present situation, have generally tended to move people in the direction of what the Greeks call "tyrannos," what we today would call strong leadership that generally comes to command structure organizations. That is certainly what we saw in management and systems theory in the 1980s. One the other hand, more recent management theory has tended to point to more transitory alliances defined as loose connections for the purposes of collaborative activity in regard to short- or medium-term projects. In other words, centralized structures in this stream of organizational theory are regarded as the antecedent model that is not appropriate to the present environment, which in that literature is beginning to be described as post-corporate.[23] Whether these proposals are right is not the point. The point is that deliberate consideration of the kind of response that is appropriate for a Christian community in the Anglican tradition of faith does not appear in this report. How much of this pluralism should be embraced, how much rejected? According to

23. See the excellent summary of the state of the debate in Limerick, Cunnington, and Crowther, *Managing the New Organisation.*

what criteria should such judgments be based? The first IATDC report, *For the Sake of the Kingdom*, did engage with these questions, but the Virginia Report seems unaware of the argument in that report. Nor is there any serious analysis of the nature of the unity that is being sought. Unity appears as a very flexible notion with meanings and uses more assumed than clarified.

## Issues in the Presenting Context

A number of issues are raised by the presenting context in the Virginia Report that require more significant analysis and critique than the report has given.

The report appears to be hierarchically focused. But is Anglicanism adequately characterized in that way? Where in this is there respect for the conciliar or synodical tradition in Anglican theology and the notion of dispersed authority? An underlying issue in the English Reformation was a conflict of instincts about the nature of authority. The need for King Henry VIII to have a divorce was simply the occasion for the expression of a conflict between Henry and the Pope that was carried on in the same "imperial" coinage. At the theological level, however, the conflict arose from a combination of a conciliar instinct together with some strands of northern European humanism that made impossible the acceptance of the centralized and singular notions of authority emerging in the new papacy. The questions of authority, a conciliar tradition, and instincts for a dispersed authority are actually quite fundamental to Anglicanism and appear to be glossed in this report.

Similarly the church as a community of the baptized is logically prior to the issue of ministry and order yet that appears not to be part of the thinking represented in this report. Nor is the way in which the church's institutions exist to serve and foster particular kinds of community life adequately examined. Yet this is a critical issue given the kind of postmodern context and the interrelationship between political and community questions that are central to the issues before the commission.

The relationship of theological truth to the wider cultural context is present but not adequately recognized. History suggests that the spirit of democracy and the conciliar conception of ecclesial life came into contact with each other in the emergence of synods in Anglicanism in North America, Australia, and elsewhere. The ECUSA Constitution follows in remarkable ways the broad outlines of the American Constitution. There was a considerable overlap in the people involved in the creation of each. In the nineteenth century, both in Canada and Australia, it was clearly the spirit of democracy that had a significant influence on the shape of the synods that eventually emerged in each of those countries.[24] That in itself raises a question that the report is directly concerned with but which it hardly unravels to any degree—namely, what is the relationship between that which occurs in, indeed may be said to be revealed in, the working of the providence of God in the events of history, on the one hand, and, on the other hand, the understanding of the character of God and of theological principles revealed in the sources of the Christian tradition, principally and supremely the Scriptures.

It is surprising and more than disappointing that the resources of the report of the first IATDC, *For the Sake of the Kingdom,* are not utilized in this report. The earlier report dealt directly with the interaction between context and gospel and addressed at some length issues raised by contemporary pluralism. There was rich material in that report on the understanding of diversity within the world-wide Anglican communities and a significant eschatological dynamic. Such a framework would have greatly assisted a discussion of the foundation and nature of institutions in the life of the church. But the Virginia Report moves in very different territory and lacks such a dynamic framework. It yields a very static view of the church, has difficulty developing an argument that connects institutional issues with the rich theological discussion of its earlier chapters, and scarcely examines the situation of Christians in the world.

Conflict is on the surface in all of this and calls for significant theological and social analysis. But the report glosses the issues that are common coin in the field of conflict resolution. In this report, conflict is to be contained and controlled by an increase in the coercive power of some of the existing institutions. There is no sense of the positive value of conflict or its creative possibilities. It would have been a great advance if the report had approached the topic with some more articulated sense of the problem as one of conflict resolution.

There is a lot of very good material in the Virginia Report. There is some rigorous theological analysis and strong argument. But in terms of assisting Anglicans to deal with the conflicts over the gender relations

---

24. On Australia, see Kaye, "Strange Birth of Anglican Synods."

in the public life of the church, it sets the discussion off on a strategy of controlling dissent and conflict. As a result it moves in a centralizing direction with a somewhat static approach to ecclesiology. It is not surprising that from its first sentence the Virginia Report conceives of the problem before Anglicans as one of a unity that is presented in static and coherence terms. It is not good enough for the task before Anglicans. It lacks a profound historical dimension in its view of Anglicanism. It fails to identify the role of the gospel imperative for Christians to live out the terms of their faith in their personal circumstances and the cultural context in which they are located. Because it fails to pay attention to this dynamic, it fails to relate this gospel imperative in the emergence of such different approaches to issues of sexuality and the role this has had in creating differences between Anglicans around the world. It lacks a serious appreciation of the background of the provincial character of Anglican ecclesiology, and it does not grapple with ways of dealing creatively with conflict. It is static in tone and does not look beyond a centralist organizational approach. It is, alas, not good enough.

# 6

## The Windsor Report: The Questions Less Asked

THE LAMBETH COMMISSION, WHICH produced the Windsor Report, was appointed because The Episcopal Church in the United States confirmed the appointment of an openly gay man as a bishop and because the Canadian church confirmed the propriety of liturgies for blessing of same-sex relationships. But the Windsor Report does not deal with these subjects. It is concerned with process. It was written by the Lambeth Commission on Communion, chaired by Robin Eames. Paragraph 26 of the report says:

> It should be clearly understood that this Commission has not been asked to continue this conversation, nor comment on or reconsider either the Lambeth Resolution or the Primates' Statement. Further serious Communion-wide discussion of the relevant issues is clearly needed as a matter of urgency, but that is not part of our mandate.

The mandate for the commission clearly stated that it was about how the Anglican Communion was to function organizationally. In this respect it carried on where the Virginia Report left off.

Having set out on this path, the report reviews the steps by which the proposal to ordain women as priests and then as bishops was promoted. It is underlined that widespread consultation took place at the time and at each stage. In contrast, the actions taken in Canada and the US followed no such consultation and indeed flew in the face of advice from the Primates' meeting. The diocese of New Westminster approved services of blessing for same-sex unions, and the Canadian General Synod affirmed the integrity and sanctity of committed adult same-sex relationships. A "divorced man openly acknowledged to be living in a sexually active and committed same sex relationship" was ordained as bishop of New Hampshire with the approval of the General Convention of ECUSA. Some bishops have intervened in other dioceses to exercise what they claim is episcopal oversight, and in the words of the Windsor Report "these developments have now contributed materially to a tit-for-tat stand-off in which, tragically in line with analogous political disasters in the wider world, each side now accuses the other of atrocities, and blames the other for the need to react further in turn."[1] These actions precipitated the crisis meeting of Primates in October 2003 and the appointment of the Lambeth Commission on Communion, which in turn produced the Windsor report.

The Report identifies six underlying issues which it believes produce the symptoms of this conflict:

1. Theological development—things change and we develop our understanding of the faith.

2. Ecclesiastical procedures were not followed.

3. *Adiaphora*—the idea that there are some things that are core and others where we can live comfortably with differences within the church.

4. Subsidiarity—that is, deciding matters at the lowest level in a hierarchy as is possible. The Canadians and Americans were wrong in their judgment on this issue.

5. Trust has been a casualty in this episode and needs to be re-built.

6. Authority—we have not worked through how the style of authority we agree about actually works, or should work.

The Windsor Report makes a number of recommendations:

1. There should be a moratorium and a period of listening.

2. An enhanced role for the Archbishop of Canterbury to "intervene" in a province and to have a council of advice to assist him in this.

3. Change the constitution of the Anglican Consultative Council to include the Primates as the Episcopal representatives and to make the elected provincial representatives more effective by being members of the provincial structures.

---

1. *Windsor Report*, par. 30.

4.  A covenant be entered into by provinces that would enhance fellowship and commonality.

In February 2005, the Primates received this report and issued a long and detailed statement. They expressed disquiet at the idea of an enhanced role for the Archbishop of Canterbury to intervene, and they set up a Panel of Reference to supervise visiting arrangements for bishops who offer Episcopal oversight to parishes who have lost confidence in their diocesan bishop. It asked the ACC to initiate a listening and study process on the sexuality issues and asked the Archbishop of Canterbury to establish a reception process, that is, a process that could monitor how the report and associated actions were being received. They also requested that ECUSA and the Canadian church voluntarily withdraw their members from the ACC until the next Lambeth Conference, save that they should be invited to make a presentation to the next meeting of the ACC.[2]

The ACC met in June 2005 and confirmed the constitutional changes and also heard the presentation from the North Americans. They reiterated the call of the Windsor Report for calm:

> 156. We call upon all parties to the current dispute to seek ways of reconciliation, and to heal our divisions. We have already indicated (paragraphs 134 and 144) some ways in which the Episcopal Church (USA) and the Diocese of New Westminster could begin to speak with the Communion in a way which would foster reconciliation. We have appealed to those intervening in provinces and dioceses similarly to act with renewed respect. (105) We would expect all provinces to respond with generosity and charity to any such actions. It may well be that there need to be formal discussions about the path to reconciliation, and a symbolic Act of Reconciliation, which would mark a new beginning for the Communion, and a common commitment to proclaim the Gospel of Christ to a broken and needy world.
>
> 157. There remains a very real danger that we will not choose to walk together. Should the call to halt and find ways of continuing in our present communion not be heeded, then we shall have to begin to learn to walk apart. We would much rather not speculate on actions that might need to be taken if, after acceptance by the primates, our recommendations are not implemented. However, we note that there are, in any human dispute, courses that may be followed: processes of mediation and arbitration; non-invitation

2. Anglican Communion, "Primates' Meeting February 2005 Communiqué."

to relevant representative bodies and meetings; invitation, but to observer status only; and, as an absolute last resort, withdrawal from membership. We earnestly hope that none of these will prove necessary. Our aim throughout has been to work not for division but for healing and restoration. The real challenge of the gospel is whether we live deeply enough in the love of Christ, and care sufficiently for our joint work to bring that love to the world, that we will "make every effort to maintain the unity of the Spirit in the bond of peace" (Eph 4. 3). As the primates stated in 2000, "to turn from one another would be to turn away from the Cross", and indeed from serving the world which God loves and for which Jesus Christ died.

The ACC also encouraged such a listening process in each Province and requested the Secretary General:

1.  to collate relevant research studies, statements, resolutions and other material on these matters from the various Provinces and other interested bodies within those Provinces

2.  to make such material available for study, discussion and reflection within each member Church of the Communion

3.  to identify and allocate adequate resources for this work, and to report progress on it to the Archbishop of Canterbury, to the next Lambeth Conference and the next meeting of this Council, and to copy such reports to the Provinces.[3]

The report draws a parallel between the ordination of women and the current issues of sexuality that is hardly sustainable. The ordination of women concerned the church coming to terms with changes in the wider society that had been in train over a period of a hundred years. Furthermore, the population of the Anglican Communion that was consulted—that is, the institutional elites—was at that time in large measure Western or Western-trained.

By contrast, the issue of sexuality has come up more quickly and at a time when the institutional voices in the communion are no longer so commonly Western. The majority of bishops are not now Western. Even within the broader cultural assumptions of Western countries, these issues are still contentious. In Canada there is a rights law that provides

3. The resolutions of the ACC are provided on the Anglican Communion web site at http://www.anglicancommunion.org/communion/acc/meetings/acc14/resolutions.cfm

the basis for changes in legal arrangements. In the U.S. different states have different patterns, and these have proved in the recent past to be highly contentious. In Australia gay and lesbian people have most but not all individual rights at law as other citizens, though marriage is reserved in Federal legislation for heterosexual relationships. In the non-Western world, the matter is extremely contentious, and in places like Nigeria it is enmeshed with the politics of relations between Christians and Muslims. Christians who appear "soft" or "Western" in these contexts are easily described by others as disloyal and foreign in their attitudes.

Sexual relations are more fundamental in the human condition generally and as a result more contentious and more complicated. What worked for the ordination of women issue may not be assumed to be appropriate or effective for homosexuality.

While process is important in terms of facilitating conflict resolution, it is not the whole story in this matter by any means. The failures at the 1998 Lambeth Conference and the terms of some of the cyber warfare going on in this matter cannot be explained simply as failures of process. They represent failures of conduct. For the ordinary Anglican watching the 1998 Lambeth Conference from outside through the public media, it was the appalling behavior and language of some of the bishops that was so embarrassing. That problem continues on the internet. Modeling love and respect is a vital part of dealing with conflict in the Christian community in any kind of structured process. If Christian people, especially organizationally prominent Christians, do not love each other, then they do not have a Christian witness to offer.

The Windsor Report and the Anglican Consultative Council looked for conversation at two levels. At the global level, time-out was called for a process of listening to various people and groups including gay and lesbian members of the church. Provinces were also asked to engage in listening and conversation on the issues of gender relations and the ACC called for a report on these province level conversations. This request to the provinces and for a report had been made before, but no report had been forthcoming. Some provinces did engage with this issue, and their reports have become available but there is hardly a flood of material and not much evidence of the circulation of any provincial reports on the web site of the Anglican Communion.[4]

---

4. See for example Office of Communication, *To Set Our Hope on Christ*.

While it is not a favorable time for openhearted conversation on such a contentious public issue, it is nonetheless a long-standing Christian obligation for Christians to listen to each other and seek to learn in all humility.

When Paul wrote to those non-listening Corinthians, he tried to make the point that God was present in their church in each member and that the contributions each brought to the life of community was a gift from God. If the church conversation was to be a participation in the divine, then the central divine quality of love was the touchstone of this utterance and listening. Speech that did not participate in that quality was just like a noisy gong or a clanging cymbal. Listening that was not patient, kind, not envious or boastful or arrogant or rude was not divinely inspired listening. Such a conversation did not necessarily lead to agreement. On the contrary, Paul told his Corinthian friends, we wait patiently and now see only dimly. For Paul the church was thus always on a pilgrimage towards the end time. Certainly Christians have had to find ways of identifying what issues are of such importance that this conversation falters, but that is a precipice that we should naturally and properly avoid as long as we can. The horizon of eternity should bring us back again and again in love and respect to the conversation with our fellow Christians.

The difficulty is that the times in which we live do not make such conversation easy, and we Anglicans have not always done well. The global environment in which we live is marked by intensity of presence and the magnification of distance. The intensity of presence is in large measure effected by the media and the internet, which brings everything into our homes instantly. But we discover that not only information about our friends and loved ones who are distant comes instantly, also information about horror, terrorist bombings, inhuman atrocities, appalling suffering from natural disasters, and human neglect also come instantly. The massacre at Columbine High comes as quickly as the photos of our grandchildren, and so we learn to distance ourselves from these horrors. We protect ourselves from such abuses of power and gross inhumanity by magnifying the distance between these things and ourselves. We isolate ourselves, and as the social scientists tell us, we look for communities in the local and the proximate made up of those more similar to ourselves. These things make conversation in a large, worldwide community like the Anglican Communion very difficult indeed.

The world is also now a more uncertain place than it used to be. Who would have thought that we might one day look back with some nostalgia for the bizarre certainties of the Cold War? Now terror is near at hand and potentially ever present. Like our predecessors in such anxious circumstances we look for more dominant leaders to protect us. The psychological furniture of de-colonization had hardly been shuffled off the stage when a new form of empire presented itself.

In their recent book *The Presidentialization of Politics*, Thomas Poguntke and Paul Webb assembled a series of studies of democratic nations and tested how far power had become more concentrated in the hands of a few or of one, even without significant changes being made in the democratic institutions of the state. They found that this process of presidentialization had advanced significantly in the United Kingdom, Germany, and Italy. It has long been an established pattern in the U.S., where there is an elected monarchy, and it is clearly a well-developed trend in Australia.

This process, they argue, is helped by the structure of the media, the formation of socio-political cleavages in society, and the internationalization of decision-making on matters that can directly affect individuals. The mass migrations of the twentieth century contribute to the formation of social cleavages. Immigrants do not entirely leave behind their own culture and habits when they settle in a new country. Among those habits are the religious traditions, so that one of the startling religious facts of the modern world is that the major religious traditions have never been in such close contact with each other. National sentiment and affections have thus become complex. This in turn means that the task of enculturation of the gospel also becomes more complex in each locality.

It is in this more complex and uncertain environment that the presidentialization of power is to be understood. It should not surprise us therefore to notice that decision-making in this context is conceived of in global terms, and that often those decisions that have implications for the accretion of structural and symbolic power are the ones for whom resources can be found. These forces also influence the way the Anglican Communion works and as such they constitute a challenge for Anglicans to discern the gospel in the face of these forces.

In this context I want to make a distinction between authority and power. Power I take to be the capacity to require action from another. The most basic instrument of power is coercion by physical force, the capacity to imprison, to punish by restriction or financial penalty. In short all those things available to the state through the law. But power moves along a scale of human conduct in relation to others to the merest relational signal that can require action. The presidentialization to which Poguntke and Webb draw attention is a matter of power. Furthermore, it is a process of the centralization of power, in their case on the political figure, Prime Minister or Chancellor. Authority, on the other hand, I take to be that source or sources to which appeal is made in order to persuade someone else within the framework of a community of some degree of shared assumptions and values. It seeks voluntary action on the basis of the individual's judgment.

The current debates in world Anglicanism display many of the elements of the presidentialization of power, and the recommendations of both the Virginia Report and the Windsor Report move significantly in this direction. The Primates were quite correct to express concern about the Windsor recommendation for an enhanced role for the Archbishop of Canterbury, which they seem to see as moving a pastoral role into a power role. The problem is that Anglicans have always had trouble with the relation between power and authority. Down through history we have been committed to a church marked by a form of dispersed and persuasive authority, but have flirted regularly with a more direct and imperial exercise of power. The Lambeth Conference resolution calling for the Archbishop of Canterbury to have power to intervene in provinces was just such a flirtation and the Primates were right to reject it when it came to them from the Windsor Report.

In Anglican history we recall that Henry VIII delivered the Church of England from the power of the Pope. The essential issue was the demand of the Pope to control aspects of life in England, a power Henry and most of his predecessors were not willing to concede. Henry asserted his independence by the exercise of just the same kind of power that the Pope had long been claiming. The Acts of Royal Supremacy, and especially the later 1662 Act of Uniformity, represent just such an exercise of power in the domestic life of the nation. At one level it represented the long tradition of lay control of the church, but it did so in a way that failed to express the underlying instinct of authority in Anglicanism, nor the wider and long tradition of common law.

William Jacob puts this point very well, and what he says has direct relevance to the task we now face in the Anglican Communion.

> It is a constitutional episcopacy in which the faithful people of God may overrule bishops, as the English parliament did in 1559 in renouncing the authority of the bishop of Rome over English dioceses and authorizing the use of the Prayer Book, against the wills of the English bishops. Constitutional synods, including lay people as well as bishops and clergy, in every diocese of every province of the Communion provide a check on the authority of any bishop or conference of bishops. Dispersed authority allows for experiment and gradual change, which takes into account the practices and views of all the people of God who owe their allegiance to dioceses in communion with one another and with the see of Canterbury.[5]

Some aspects of the Windsor Report embody unwelcome flirtations with power as the category to deal with the problems in the Communion and sideline important elements in Anglican tradition and sentiment about the nature of the church.

The Windsor Report envisages that the sexuality issue will be debated in the provinces and that the Anglican Communion responsibility is to provide a process to contain or control conflict between provinces. In one sense the primary debate about gender relations does lie with the provinces, because the question is so embedded in the cultural context in which we each live. Furthermore, this discussion involves personal issues for us all that require of us openness, generosity, and humility that need to be exercised at close quarters. The globalizing trends to personal disengagement and the centralizing of power as a solution to local conflict do not assist. In fact they represent the dark powers that corrupt the church.

There are in reality different elements at work in the provincial debate from those relevant to the global interactions. The debate in the provinces is both more immediately personal and also set within more established and powerful institutional frameworks. It is more personal because those involved continue to live with each other in greater proximity. In the way of the long tradition of Anglican ecclesiology, the judicature is more secure and the capacity for more effective and well agreed discipline of clergy and bishops is more substantial. Furthermore, for the same reason of proximity, a greater cross-section of the church community can be actively involved. The debate will affect individuals in the church quite personally and directly as will any decisions made.

---

5. Jacob, *Making of the Anglican Church*, 300.

At the global level, the pattern is quite different. The issue there is not about the actions of individuals but the actions of provinces. The conflict focused on Gene Robinson had to do not with his personal actions but with the institutional action of the province, ECUSA, in electing him to be a bishop and in confirming that election. Individuals are indeed personally affected, but the conflict is about institutional relationships.

This contrast is not by any means absolute. Even with the more obviously power-shaped relations between nation-states, the personal is not totally excluded. The Anglican Communion is not a federation of nation-states. It is a voluntary association of voluntary associations, and as a consequence the nature of the power that is possible is distinctly different. There may be ecclesiastical analogies to a trade embargo, but no one imagines that in the Anglican Communion anyone can physically invade another province and by force of arms compel compliance. The very nature of the communities involved, let alone impulses of Christian vocation, mean that this sort of power is simply not conceivable in the present conflict.

Even within a province the power to require actions from others is not at all straightforward. In a curious way, Richard Hooker has a helpful point on this even though he wrote at a time when the power of the sword was not only available to the church but was actively used.

Hooker[6] faced the problem of trying to interpret the situation of a Christian nation in which the church was coextensive with the nation. So his principal challenge was how to interpret the royal supremacy in England in a theologically satisfactory way. It was not a straightforward challenge. But he was also faced with the situation of different nations having different national Christian polities and practices. He thus also faced the issue of catholicity for the world of his day—that is, Christian Europe.

These are issues that in one sense move in the opposite direction to the issues facing Anglicans today. We have multiple traditions of Christianity within secular nations, or in some cases in Muslim or Hindu nations. For us, the Christian nation is not a category in considering catholicity. Nonetheless, underlying Hooker's approach to these questions was a conception of power that seems to me to point to a theological approach that sheds some light on our situation.

6. See Gascoigne, "Unity of Church and State Challenged," and "Church and State United."

The principal material on power is in book 8 of the *Lawes*, though there are other passages that touch on this issue, not least the Introduction, book 1 on law, and also book 6. However, it is in book 8 that Hooker comes to the issue directly. We should note that the new Dublin manuscripts used in the Folger edition change the prominence given to aspects of the exposition in this book. In brief, the effect is to show that the correct arrangement of the chapters gives more prominence to chapter 2 than was the case in, say, the Keble edition, and also that the Old Testament material is, in Stephen McGrade's terms, corroborative rather than probative.[7] The argument proper begins in chapter 2 with an extraordinarily compact statement of the argument. So much so that I quote it at length:

> Without order there is no living in publique societie, because the want thereof is the mother of confusion, wherupon division of necessitie followeth, and out of division inevitable destruction. The Apostle therefore giving instruction to publique societies requireth that all thinges be orderley done. Order can have no place in things unless it be setled amongst the person that shall by office be conversant about them. And if thinges or persons be ordered, this doth implie that they are distiquished by degrees. For order is a graduall disposition. The whole world consisting of partes so manie so different is by this only thing upheld, he which framed them hath set them in order. Yea the very deitie it self both keepeth and requireth for ever this to be kept as a law, that wheresoever there is a coagmentation of many, the lowest be knitt to the highest by that which being interjacent may cause each to cleave unto the other and so all to continue one. This order of thinges and persons in publique societies is the worke of politie and the proper instrument thereof in every degree is power, power being that abilitie which we have of our selves to receive from others for performance of any action. If the action which we are to perform be conversant about matter of meer religion, the power of performing it is then spirituall. And if that power be such as hath not any other to overule it, we terme it dominion or power supreme, so far as the bounds thereof do extend.[8]

Hooker sets his notion of power within a framework of order in society. No society exists without order, and order implies different degrees of

---

7. McGrade, "Introduction to Book VIII," 6A:359.

8. Hooker, *Lawes* 8.2.1 (*Works* 3:331).

power according to the place in the social order of those exercising that power. Thus, for Hooker, power is dependent on social order.

That social order is itself based upon the agreement of the "multitude" comprising the society. Every multitude has power over itself, and even hereditary kings hold their power in dependency on the whole. In chapter 3, Hooker goes on to develop his argument with a series of five questions as to how power is held. His questions and answers are, in summary, as follows:

1.  By what right? From God through men in the form of a contract.

2.  After what sort? In dependence on the whole body politic.

3.  In what measure? According to law.

4.  With what conveniencie? Particular powers for expedition of action and to avoid confusion.

5.  According to what example? The example of Israel is used and differences with the Christian Church noted together with the differences among christian nations.

This broad conception of power was the basis of the qualifications that Hooker placed on the royal supremacy—the ultimate power in England and operating over all members of the nation. Within this framework three very significant qualifications are placed on the royal supremacy. First, it is qualified by the universal and supreme sovereignty of God. The mandate of the royal supremacy comes from God through men—that is, through the "multitude" that has power over itself. Also Christ's lordship is limitless in respect to the world and mankind, whereas that of the crown is limited to the nation in which the crown is held. Further, the crown exercises a lordship that deals only with externals, whereas Christ's lordship works also inwardly by grace in the individual and in the church.

Secondly, the royal supremacy is qualified in relation to law. This emphasis has precedent in English political theory,[9] even though it might not immediately appear to be the case in the actual operation of Tudor politics. It is more likely that Hooker is describing what he wishes were so more than what was actually the case—what we might today call "performative discourse."

---

9. For example, in Fortescue, *On the Laws and Governance of England*.

Thirdly, the royal supremacy is qualified in relation to the community. This qualification is consonant with Hooker's views on consensus[10] and the contractarian aspect of his understanding of society. He gives a place for an inclusive parliament on the grounds that it would be unjust for one part of the community to make laws for the rest. Not only the foundation but also the exercise of the royal supremacy is dependent on those other parts of the order of society.

In this context power is thus a matter of exercising that capacity given by the place a person occupies in the order of society. The order itself gains strength as the adjacent parts "cleave" together.[11] This is a very particular conception of society and its unity. It is shaped by a graduated order that yields power for those who inhabit the order because the order itself derives its potency by it being the creature of the multitude and serving the multitude's coherent life. It is notable also that Hooker envisages a hierarchy of order that is relatively flat. Institutional distance is the enemy of community and has the effect of disempowering those with responsibility for the social structure.

The Windsor Report is looking for some means of control. A capacity to make effective decisions on issues in conflict between provinces. This strategy of containment calls for some kind of power to require actions of others. Hooker's analysis makes clear that such power derives its potency from its position within a structured and fairly coherent community. Hooker has in mind a nation that exists under law within a sovereign territory. Even in these circumstances he sees that the community that inhabits this state operates generally on the basis of the acceptance by the members of the terms of their "contract." They internalize the structure and its authority and act accordingly.

10. See Grislis, "Role of Consensus."

11. The text is famously quoted in the bull *Unam Sanctam* of Boniface VIII, though there it is used to justify papal superiority over the secular (Philip the Fair of France): "For, according to the Blessed Dionysius, it is a law of the divinity that the lowest things reach the highest place by intermediaries. Then, according to the order of the universe, all things are not led back to order equally and immediately, but the lowest by the intermediary, and the inferior by the superior. Hence we must recognize the more clearly that spiritual power surpasses in dignity and in nobility any temporal power whatever, as spiritual things surpass the temporal." See Luscombe, "'Lex Divinitatis' in the Bull 'Unam Sanctam.'" Hooker, on the other hand, uses the text, whose authenticity he seems not to question, to argue for the coherence of the whole.

In pursuing a strategy of constraint, the Windsor Report must necessarily look for some form of contract between the members that could be the beginning of the development of some kind of power. The category adopted by the Windsor Report is a "covenant." The term has rhetorically useful biblical resonances. One can only wonder about this choice in the light of the covenant initiated by God in the redemption of the people of Israel from Egypt. This covenant yielded in political terms an "amphictomy," that is to say a coalition of semi-autonomous tribes held together by a common religious vocation and united in action from time to time by the need to deal with a common external threat. The move away from this theocratic and prophetic model was regarded as a form of apostasy, because it was seen as a rejection of the divine rule.

At the last supper Jesus associated his death (his blood) with this covenant. That association is embedded into the continuing memory of the last supper in the "Lord's Supper" of the Christian church. That continuing memory of the covenant is in some contrast with the language of fulfillment in relation to the nation, temple, and land. It is striking that the law as fulfilled in Christ had more persistent significance for Christians. The prophetic preference for theocracy which is seen in the church in the rule of the risen Christ is the disturbing absence in the Windsor Report covenant proposal.

The Windsor Report moves to its strategy of constraint and control before clarifying the nature of the community within which that constraint is to be exercised. If the nature of a global entity in a religious tradition like Anglicanism had been analyzed first, then the kind of restraint and power that was appropriate in such a community could have been better enterprised.

Gore Vidal and George Bush are both citizens of the U.S. and live within that context despite fundamentally disagreeing on a range of quite-important matters. Any category such as English, Nigerian, Kenyan, Malaysian, or New Zealand, will have within it the space and capacity for the successful cohabitation of very significant differences. The question before Anglicans is not dissimilar. What kinds of difference can successfully cohabit within the category Anglican? The answer to that question cannot be whatever is politically decided by this particular generation of office holders. Anglicanism has a history, a story. The current participants do not act on their own uniqueness; they act out of the Anglican tradition of faith, or at least they should.

What is left begging in the argument of the Windsor Report is any developed account of what kind of entity or thing the Anglican Communion actually is. Neither the Virginia Report nor the Windsor Report confront the question of what in Anglican ecclesiological terms we are to make of the Anglican Communion. By default the material assumption is that it is, or should be, some kind of universal church. But it is far from clear what that might mean in terms of the Anglican tradition of Christian faith.

This failure to address such a fundamental issue has probably contributed to the unreasoned adoption of a constraint strategy in dealing with conflict. A more open address to the problem might have allowed more imagination to be deployed in shaping direct conflict resolution strategies in relation to the substantive issue of the place of homosexuality in the public life of the church. It might also have more easily opened up the priority of global community building activities such as the now apparently abandoned world Anglican Gathering.

How to respond to cultural forces shaping relations between the sexes is as much a challenge in Nigeria as it is in North America. Both Nigerian and North-American Anglicans must deal with decisions at two levels. The first relates to what we think ourselves and thus how we will personally live in relation to our own and other individuals' sexuality. The second relates to what the church ought to do in this area. This is a different question because it involves community and institutional dimensions. The very existence of free and open dissent within a community on any matter is evidence not only that the church is a mixed congregation, but also that our Christian fellowship is not dependent on all agreeing on everything that happens to come up.

Two things make this debate both important and challenging. The subject matter draws to the surface differences of theological conviction about which we feel very strongly. Strength of conviction has both intellectual and emotional elements, and we may well therefore find ourselves deeply challenged personally by a public engagement with each other on this subject. Secondly, the subject matter touches very directly not just the personal circumstances of many in our church but also their sense of who they are. As a consequence, our discussion could be deeply hurtful for some, particularly our gay and lesbian brothers and sisters in Christ, or it could be personally affirming. How we conduct this conversation is thus in itself a vital part of the process we are engaged in. It will make a great difference for both our personal identities and our corporate life as a Christian community. Finding ways of affirming each other while confronting deep disagreements is never easy.

It seems to me that there are three elements in making decisions about matters of Christian faith and life, and all of them are about attending to the voice of the living God. They are listening for that voice through the experience of our own lives, through the deposit of faith, and through the life and experience of the Christian community.

In the end we each have to make our own decision on these matters but this conversation is an invitation to share in a corporate activity for the church community. But the way in which we do that arises out all the contingent circumstances of our own personal experience of the God and Father of our Lord Jesus Christ. It arises out our experience of prayer. It arises out of our own habitual responses to the touch of the Holy Spirit.

Of course, as Christians we do not live in isolation and we do not invent our Christianity for ourselves. We are the recipients of this faith and are defined as Christians by the faith that was delivered to the church through the apostles. This is the deposit of faith.

There is much discussion in this area about scripture and of specific texts such as Rom 1:24–27. Part of the argument is about how a text such as this is to be understood in the cultural and linguistic context of its day and in the otherwise discernible views of the writer. Then there is the issue of how this text relates to other texts that seem to speak of a more inclusive view, and further what relative force is to be given to one text as compared with another.

But I suspect that a more fundamental question has to do with the way in which we think scripture actually works in exercising its appropriate authority for us. Are we not more likely to answer questions about particular texts in the light of a general view of the whole of scripture in the framework of what we might call our creedal beliefs? As one who spent the first fifteen years of my professional life in the university teaching the New Testament, what I took from that fifteen year preparation was not specific texts on particular topics but an overall framework of belief and a sense of the landscape and flow of the Christian revelation. It seems to me that a key issue in coming to some conclusion about sexuality is an understanding of how our sense of the Christian faith is shaped by and shapes the way we respond to the ongoing influence of scripture in our formation. I find myself having to reach beyond the texts to the dynamics of the faith that has been so created and formed by constant intercourse with the whole of scripture. This takes much patient and persistent listening.

Decision-making thus involves asking what the Spirit says to us and what the deposit of faith says to us. Such decisions always involve elements of judgment, issues of wisdom and insight. The church as the community of God's people is not just a repository of such wisdom and insight in others, it is a community marked by the presence of God through the gifts that are given. Just as it is proper and necessary to say that God is present to us in the testimony of the Spirit and in the voice of the gospel, so it is also true to say that God is present in the community of the faithful. Thus listening to each other is another way in which we attend to God as we seek out our Christian responsibility. The conversation Anglicans are invited to embark upon is itself a theological activity, a means of attending to the wisdom of God in each other, and thus to be enterprised with fear and trembling, almost as a kind of prayer.

Christian ethical discourse is not an algorithm, a calculation of pluses and minuses. It is a question of seeking guidance from the God who has called us. It is therefore always a matter of walking by faith, and doing so in the present. Just as we can find it easy to see the oddity of the views of our Victorian predecessors, so we should remember that our successors in turn will find it just as easy to see the oddity of our own stumbling conclusions.

In relation to the action of the church, it seems to me that there are four key questions with which the church must grapple in this area.

1.  The liturgical blessing of same sex relationships.

2.  The ordination of people in open committed same-sex relationships.

3.  Our relations with other Anglican churches who do not share our view on these matters.

4.  What do we think ought to be the legal framework in the country in which we live?

How we handle these matters will be a test of our Christian integrity and faith.

# 7

# Will the Windsor Process Lead to the Precipice?

THE WINDSOR REPORT SUGGESTED a way forward that became known as the Windsor Process. The central item was to develop a covenant. This process continued the direction set in the Virginia Report and the Windsor Report itself of looking for a mechanism to gain compliance from delinquent provinces. Significant efforts were made to keep this process transparent by consulting and publishing progress reports. Even so the range of people engaged in this process was still relatively narrow. The Covenant Design Group issued two drafts, and they appear to be looking very hard for a final document that will gain wide support. They have not been helped in this by the Primates meeting, which took up the first draft and used it preemptively with The Episcopal Church. It is clear that there are a number of residual political currents at work in this whole arena: hangover colonial attitudes, various forms of imperial mentalities ideological and dispositional, and the simple power of resources such as money, information control, numbers, and media access. In amongst these not-so-attractive forces are also reasonable people trying to do good.

It would be a mistake to think that the Windsor Process was the only game in town. Consecrations of bishops to serve in other provinces continues, a large conference is advertised as if it might be an alternative function to the Lambeth Conference, and the Lambeth Conference continues to develop along the lines of it being a conference rather than a putative parliament. In the midst of these, the final report of the Inter-Anglican Theological and Doctrinal Commission entitled *Communion Conflict and Hope* was published, which finally put a few theological question marks against the Virginia/Windsor stream of consciousness.

Will this Windsor Process lead Anglicanism to a precipice? That depends on what you think a precipice might be. Will it lead to organizational fragmentation in World Anglicanism? Quite possibly. Will that be a precipice of any significance? That will depend on what criteria are brought to bear. If one has in mind concepts like some sort of visible unity and coherence, then it could well be a significant precipice. But Anglicans have multiplied organizational arrangements before, such as during the missionary expansion in the nineteenth century. It might have had some down sides, but it was hardly fatal. What if we applied the test expressed by Tertullian: "It is our care of the helpless, our practice of loving kindness that brands us in the eyes of many of our opponents. 'Only look,' they say, 'look how they love one another,'"[1] which of course is simply a rendition of Jesus' last words to his disciples, "by this everyone will know that you are my disciples, if you have love for one another."[2] This test as to what is a precipice in this context is not organizational. It is something much more profound. It is whether in whatever happens these Anglicans love one another as Christ has loved them. So is that precipice already in front of us?

It certainly is an issue in the Listening Process. That process was asked for both in terms of listening to the experience of gay and lesbian members of the church, and also in terms of the debates about these issues in the provinces. These two are not the same, but neither are they separable. Listening to the testimony of fellow Christians is part of the theological endeavor. It is part of the process of attending to the voice of God in the church. Listening to the experience of gay and lesbian people is also part of the pastoral role of the church to care for all in the church, but especially minorities and dissenters. In the context of public dispute in the church about sexuality, there is clearly a responsibility for listening to the experience of gay and lesbian Christians. How that happens in a way that is constructive and manifests the love which marks us out to be the disciples of Christ is not by any means easy to see in general terms. Such a process can easily give an area of personal life a degree if public attention which would not necessarily be welcomed by some gay and lesbian members of the church. When such a process is so publicly linked to disputes and conflict in the church it could very easily simply make gay and lesbian members scapegoats for these conflicts. Listening on the

---

1. Tertullian, *Apology*, chapter 39, quoted from Roberts, *Ante-Nicene Fathers*, 3:46.
2. John 13:35.

policy question in the church is a challenge for all in the church, especially those who come with already held strong opinions one way or the other.

A valuable resource is provided on the Anglican Communion web-site (http://www.aco.org/listening/index.cfm) of guidelines for such listening and for the cooperative development of a study guide. The site also contains summary reports from the provinces on the listening process. These are somewhat variable. Some report on the theological debates and others only on the process of listening to gay and lesbian members of the church. Unfortunately the authors of these summaries are not identified and so the reports are not as valuable as they might be. In effect they cannot be relied upon in a time of contention. Nonetheless the site shows serious commitment to openness and inclusion in this process. What will be made of it in due course is not clear. It is clear from the information on this site that there is a long way to go in approaching widespread understanding amongst Anglicans and also any general clarity about the prevailing views in the Provinces.

The Anglican Communion web site also provides a copy of a report of a consultation held apparently from 1999 to 2003. After the Lambeth Conference in 1998 the Archbishop of Canterbury called together eleven bishops from around the world to consult together. Their report was in fact a form of the more general listening process later put in train. The short report registers continuing disagreement on the issues but a remarkable testimony to growth in understanding and respect. They list a number of things they were able to agree upon and three which they were not. They also record what they saw as the fruit of their conversations. "While our differences remain, the relationships between us have been strengthened and deepened. We have gained in mutual respect, affection, and appreciation of one another as followers of Jesus and fellow bishops. Our Conversations have strengthened and clarified our differing convictions, not diluted them. They have helped us to understand others' views, and their roots, more fully."[3] This is a remarkable achievement and could have well been extended more widely and involved members more directly in conflict. It has the marks of conflict resolution processes for which the IATDC called in their document of September 2007.[4]

---

3. Anglican Consultative Council, "Final Report," 6.

4. IATDC, "Responding to a proposal of a covenant," section 5: "Bringing theology to bear in situations of conflict."

The Windsor Process has also involved the creation of a reference panel to provide advice on alternative episcopal arrangements made where parishes in a diocese, or dioceses in a province, have difficulties of conscience in accepting their bishop's or Metropolitan's ministry. There have been a small number of references to this panel but little has emerged from it. It clearly is not where people think the action should be. It does not for instance have the resources for serious conflict resolution processes to be introduced into such disagreements.

The most active focus of the Windsor process has been the search for a suitable form of covenant. In March 2005, the Joint Standing Committee of Primates meeting and the ACC published a document "Towards an Anglican Covenant"[5] and in May 2006 a Covenant Design Group was established and published its first report in February 2007.

The timetable for the covenant process was initially set out in The Windsor Report in very general terms. It envisaged the adoption of a simple and short domestic "communion law" in each province to implement the covenant. The five stages were: approval of a draft by the primates, submission to the churches and ACC for consultation and reception, final approval by primates, legal authorization by each church, and solemn signing by the primates. The Windsor Report timetable did not mention a role for the Lambeth conference, but the Primates in 2005 commended the covenant proposal "as a project that should be given further consideration in the Provinces of the Communion between now and the Lambeth Conference 2008. In addition, we ask the Archbishop of Canterbury to explore ways of implementing this."[6] Some consultation took place and informed the work of the Covenant Design Group. But the decision making process listed in the Windsor Report would inevitably take something like six to nine years, depending on when the decision making bodies of the provinces actually met.

The March 2006 consultation report for the Joint Standing Committee set out a more precise phased development: an initial drafting period (1 year), a period of further testing (3–5 years) and an implementation period of 2–3 years. This would be six years at a minimum (i.e., by 2012) and nine years at the upper end (i.e., by 2015). The timetable in the Primates meeting communiqué envisages further consultation after Lambeth and

5. See Anglican Consultative Council, "Towards an Anglican Covenant."
6. "Primates' meeting communiqué February 2005," para 9. I.01

a final text for ACC-14. On the current pattern of ACC meetings, that would mean 2008, earlier than the earliest date envisaged by the consultation document for the Joint Standing Committee. Clearly the timetable has been developing and apparently accelerating; but not enough for the Primates meeting, since they felt constrained to anticipate the covenant with some compliance action of their own in February 2007.

The Covenant Design Group (CDG) published its first report in February 2007 and a draft text for a covenant called the Nassau draft.[7] The report envisaged a dual track approach. The text of a covenant should be developed that in the appropriate way should go to the Provinces for consideration, leading to adoption of a final text through the relevant processes of the Provincial decision-making bodies. In the meantime, the CDG suggested there should be some general agreement to the outline shape of a covenant.

The CDG also set out the principles that influenced their work in developing this first draft. They had tried to give expression to "what may be considered authentic Anglicanism." Furthermore, the text was "meant to be robust enough to express clear commitment in those areas of Anglican faith about which there has been most underlying concern in recent events" while being faithful to what has been received. Nothing in the covenant can be said to be "new." Three times the report underlines that the covenant text brings nothing new but rather represents the faith Anglicans have received and expresses a commitment to inter-dependent life.

The final clause of the Nassau draft covenant provided the compliance material. Each church is to commit itself

1.  in essential matters of common concern, to have regard to the common good of the Communion in the exercise of its autonomy, and to support the work of the Instruments of Communion with the spiritual and material resources available to it.

2.  to spend time with openness and patience in matters of theological debate and discernment to listen and to study with one another in order to comprehend the will of God.

3.  to seek with other members, through the Church's shared councils, a common mind about matters of essential concern, consistent with the Scriptures, common standards of faith, and the canon law of our churches.

7. See CDG, "Anglican Covenant Draft."

4. to heed the counsel of our Instruments of Communion in matters which threaten the unity of the Communion and the effectiveness of our mission. While the Instruments of Communion have no juridical or executive authority in our Provinces, we recognize them as those bodies by which our common life in Christ is articulated and sustained, and which therefore carry a moral authority which commands our respect.

5. to seek the guidance of the Instruments of Communion, where there are matters in serious dispute among churches that cannot be resolved by mutual admonition and counsel:

   a. by submitting the matter to the Primates Meeting

   b. if the Primates believe that the matter is not one for which a common mind has been articulated, they will seek it with the other instruments and their councils

   c. finally, on this basis, the Primates will offer guidance and direction.

6. We acknowledge that in the most extreme circumstances, where member churches choose not to fulfill the substance of the covenant as understood by the Councils of the Instruments of Communion, we will consider that such churches will have relinquished for themselves the force and meaning of the covenant's purpose, and a process of restoration and renewal will be required to re-establish their covenant relationship with other member churches.

Although couched in convoluted and indirect language these clauses mean that where a province finds itself in a minority of one as decided by the "Instruments" it will be excluded from the covenant.

The process of covenant formation had itself been enrolled in the political aspects of the conflict over homosexuality in the public life of the church. This became apparent at the meeting of Covenant Design Group when it met in Nassau in January 2007. There was pressure at the meeting for a very rapid adoption of a covenant in order to prevent further "innovations." It was being suggested that the Primates at their meeting in Dar es Salaam in February 2007 would declare that they were to be the principal interpreters and enforcers of the covenant. In the communiqué of their February 2007 meeting, the Primates said that the way forward was to be the recommendations of the Windsor Report as interpreted by the Primates' statement at Dromantine.[8] Nevertheless, in February 2007 in Dar es Salaam, the Primates meeting clearly did not regard the Nassau draft covenant document as setting out a broad outline to be refined later. On the contrary, they took a specific clause in the draft text and used it to legitimate their extraordinary actions in relation to The Episcopal Church. They seem to have thought that the American situation was so urgent that they could not wait for a final version of the covenant to come and so they offered a foretaste of what interpretation and enforcement of any covenant might look like. They called for the establishment of a Pastoral Council and a Primatial Vicar in the life of The Episcopal Church. This was an attempt to establish a joint operation of the Primates within a particular Province that would have some decision-making powers in relation to the recognition of pastoral care for churches within that province. The Pastoral Council was thus a clear incursion into the life of a province, and it carried no real guarantees that the international interventions in the ordered life of The Episcopal Church by some of these same Primates would cease. It was simply hoped that they would. It looked very like a one-way bargain, and it was delivered with the language of threats.

The Primates also demanded assurances from the House of Bishops of The Episcopal Church, which, under the constitution of that church, the House does not have the authority to provide. Furthermore they set a deadline of September 2007 for compliance. This was not related to the covenant. It implied a role for the Primates meeting, which was not supported by any decision of any body that could be imagined to have any authority to make such a decision. One can at least say that it was a very distinct initiative. Political observers saw it as a grab for power. How far it expressed respect for the polity of The Episcopal Church, or had some reasonable connection with traditional Anglican provincial ecclesiology is very hard if not impossible to see.[9]

However, as in many things one incident should not be regarded as the permanent view of this group. The deadline for The Episcopal Church bishops' response came and went, and then a process of assessment was established with a group of people to advise on the matter. It will all take time, and time is one of the most valuable commodities in this crisis, because it gives space for more mature reflection than came out of Dar

8. See Anglican Communion, "Primates' Meeting February 2005 Communiqué."

9. See the account in Grieb, *Interpreting the Proposed Anglican Covenant.*

es Salaam. Perhaps this adventure by the Primates will come to be seen as having been a good thing because it highlighted a potential problem. In any case, the St. Andrews draft covenant published in January 2008 reflects a rejection of this kind of action by the Primates.

The most significant changes in the St. Andrews text are to the last section, which is where the institutional action resides. The Covenant Design Group also continues with their more measured timetable. They plan to consider responses from around the Communion and the Lambeth Conference and then to review the development of this whole project. The Group presented plans for developing the process to the March meeting of the Joint Standing Committee of the ACC and the Primates.

In the St. Andrews text, the tone is quite different. Instead of a province receiving "mutual admonition and counsel" they are to be invited to take part in "mediated conversations" and to "receive a request" from one of the "Instruments." Any primary role for the Primates is eclipsed and replaced with a multi-faceted consultative process that includes the provinces, the "Instruments" and the Commissions of the Communion. Furthermore, it appears that new commissions could be created perhaps specifically in relation to a matter under consideration, as suggested by the IATDC in September 2006.[10] There is a detailed outline of consultations with a final appeal to the ACC. The new text also specifically recognizes the autonomy of the provinces and repeats the Nassau statement that the "Instruments" have no legislative, executive or judicial authority in the provinces.

These changes in the text of the draft covenant indicate significant movement towards a more traditional Anglican ecclesiology with the province in a privileged position and the global institutions existing to serve the mission of the provinces.

The changes in the text are reasonably significant and are clearly to be welcomed as a response to the realities of the life and tradition in worldwide Anglicanism. They leave unresolved the relationship between the covenant and the ACC, which is the only body with a constitution approved by the provinces and therefore with any claim to a significance in worldwide Anglicanism that has been agreed to by the constituent bodies of the Communion. They also leave unanswered the relationship of the covenant to the invitation list to the Lambeth Conference. As a personal

10. IATDC, "Responding to a proposal of a covenant—October 2006," section 5.

activity of the Archbishop of Canterbury, such a conference of bishops should probably be as inclusive as possible, including not only the uniate church bishops and moderators as at present, but perhaps also other Anglican groups since split off from the official Anglican Communion as defined by the constitution of the ACC.

On a more mundane note, will clause 3.2.1 of the St. Andrews draft covenant, which calls on provinces to support the work of the "Instruments" with spiritual and material resources, have an impact on those provinces that have for many years declined to pay their allocated budget contribution to the Anglican Communion?

This draft covenant is light years away from the draft offered in the Windsor Report, but if it is to gain the support of all the provinces then it has a good deal further to go. That simply goes to show that the idea of a covenant of the type envisaged in the Windsor Report did not carry enough weight out of the Anglican tradition, nor enough awareness of the realities of life in the provinces to be a viable way forward. The question still remains as to whether this strategy of containment wrapped up in a covenant is in any case the appropriate way forward for Anglicans. The fact that the Windsor Process is by no means the only game in town at the moment rather suggests that the core of the matter has not yet been addressed successfully.

African bishops continue to consecrate bishops for episcopal work in the U.S. outside of and indeed in direct conflict with the official structures of The Episcopal Church. Some of the African Primates have been actively involved in these consecrations, claiming they were compelled by their conscience to act in this way. These same Primates took part in making judgments on and demanding changes from the North American churches at the Dar es Salaam meeting of Primates. The Primates meetings have consistently been generous and modest in their comments on these cross-border episcopal incursions, even though they are clearly contrary to the canons and order of the North American churches and also, in most cases, to the terms of the constitutions of the provinces of those Primates making the incursions. The pattern of these actions does not readily appear to be adequately straightforward.

On an altogether different level, the final Kuala Lumpur Report of the Inter-Anglican Theological and Doctrinal Commission was published in February 2008. This commission has been meeting on and off since 2001, and their report, *Communion, Conflict and Hope*, takes up the issues of the nature of the Anglican Communion. While it takes up the work of its predecessor, the Virginia Report, it moves in a significantly different direction. In part III of the report, it argues for a highly consultative approach to communion theology and gives an account of its consultations over the previous seven years. Part I gives a general introduction and indicates that the central theological account of communion offered by the Commission is provided in Part II.

This theological account of the Anglican Communion begins with a reminder of the fallibility of the church and the differences within the church that inevitably come from attempts to live faithfully in different cultural locations. Conflicts and differences are noted in the early period of church history. "These struggles were often overlaid with the all too human elements of power and prestige, ambition and pride. At a time of rapid growth in the church, the life of the community had the usual elements of moral failure, conflict, mistaken paths, as well as the resilient impulse to be faithful to Christ, to be led by the Spirit."[11]

The report refers back to the earlier IATDC report *For the Sake of the Kingdom* and its treatment of pluralism and diversity. The tenor of the report is less static than the Virginia Report and embraces difference and conflict as part of the Christian vocation in the church. It is in this context that they suggest that the church is a "school for Christian virtues."[12] The report speaks in more dynamic terms of communion and in terms of love rather than unity. This emphasis more readily recognizes the inevitable differences and conflicts evident in the history of the church. Unity easily slides into agreement defined in my terms and thus to uniformity. Love speaks more directly to the obligation Christians have to each other across differences. Catholicity becomes a more important consideration in this line of thought, and the Commission develops this notion from and for the local.[13] In that context the report draws attention to the provincial character of Anglican ecclesiology:

> Traditional Anglican structures have developed little beyond provincial level. That has reflected an underlying provincial ecclesiology of disciplined order sufficient to provide a ministry of word and sacraments that is both catholic and apostolic. It also embod-

11. IATDC, *Communion, Conflict and Hope,* ¶ 32.

12. Ibid., ¶ 52.

13. Ibid., ¶ 45f.

ied a practical recognition of the limits of workable connection. This is reflected in the persistent refusal of successive Lambeth Conferences to see themselves as a disciplinary body and their affirmations of provincial autonomy. As a consequence when we have had to deal with global Communion issues of order we have not had extensive ecclesiological precedent. Our history has not prepared us to handle such conflicts with confidence.[14]

It is not surprising that in this context the Commission underlines that the present circumstances of Anglicans and the Anglican Communion are novel and that inevitably differences and conflict will arise. Such conflict always involves pain and puzzlement, though when handled creatively it can be a gift from God. Such a conflicted situation that calls for enduring love must be worked out in the light of the eschatological hope of the Christian. They declare that "this hope will not permit the fallibility which we bring to handling our conflicts to be the last word."[15]

This is a very different account of the church from that found in the Virginia Report. It presents as more dynamic, more closely attuned to the reality of church life as reflected in the New Testament documents and the history of the church; it sets this fallibility into the heart of an eschatological hope that provides the dynamic for love and the growth of Christian virtues in the church. One has the feeling in this report of a much more immanent sense of the divine presence in suffering, crucifixion, and resurrection than emerged from the Virginia or Windsor reports.

It is not surprising therefore that the Commission sees its argument as presenting something of a contrary voice to the direction of the Windsor Process.

> If the outcome of the Windsor process should result in some definitive centralisation of the Communion then one function of this report may be to constitute an appraisal of that development. As the 1948 document put it: "It may be said that authority of this (dispersed) kind is much harder to understand and obey than authority of a more imperious character. This is true and we glory in the appeal which it makes to faith". Perhaps it is not that dispersed authority in the present circumstances has been tried and found

14. Ibid., ¶ 49.
15. Ibid., ¶ 51.

to fail: it is that is has been found to be too hard—and so not tried
for long enough![16]

The appearance of this report highlights the relative absence of a strong theological voice in the Windsor process. It also illustrates the need to take time. Anglicans world wide are a vast and scattered community. To imagine that major changes in the tradition such as those involved in the Windsor process can be made in such a hurry by a select group lacks both sense and credibility. It also lacks a gospel sense of patience in the light of the presence of God in the life of the church.

~

The need for patience and therefore time is clear from the manifest difficulties of mutual understanding, and in the heat of debate, loss of respect across differences. The depth of the divide can be seen in the terms used in the debate. Groups began to take to themselves and gave to their opponents descriptions that assumed a conclusion to the debate. As a result, neither could see themselves in the designations they were given by others. *Orthodox* means my interpretation over against yours. *Liberal* means having little or no significant connection with the truth of the gospel. *Open* means hospitable to all rather than closed to particular categories of people. *Instruments of unity* means the only mechanisms for maintaining coherence and belonging in the Anglican Communion, or at least the only means worth talking about. And *Anglican* is used as if it is entirely fluid in meaning and at all points requiring adjectival qualification.

The reality is that there is a discernible Anglican history and theological tradition, and there have always been arguments about the border areas of that tradition. Those arguments have also gone through apocalyptic phases, as do many conflicts in communities. One very interesting aspect of both the development of the proposed covenant and also the terms of the GAFCON conference is that as time passes moderation and even some modesty of ambition seems to be emerging. GAFCON is just one rather large and public event in a series of the sorts of events that have surrounded Lambeth Conferences for at least the last fifty years.

---

16. Ibid., ¶ 18. The internal quotation is from the Committee Report on "The Anglican Communion" in *Lambeth Conference 1948*, 85.

There is a nice irony in this particular cycle as compared with the first Lambeth Conference.[17] Some English bishops refused to attend the first conference for fear that it would attempt some legislative action. Some bishops in 2008 seem to be refusing to attend the Lambeth Conference on the grounds that it will not attempt some legislation on current issues. The English bishops in 1867 turned out to be mistaken. The conference turned out to be a conference, not a parliament, and apart from a few lapses that have eventually collapsed it has steadfastly refused to move from that consultative role. It will be important for the way Anglicans remain in connection with each other around the world to assess what this session of conferencing means for Anglicanism and whether GAFCON turns out to be a conference to encourage or a stepping stone to the consolidation of division.

17. See Chapman, "Where Is It All Going?"

# 8

## Lambeth—A Conference Re-discovered?

Two quite powerful forces have come together to make the 2008 Lambeth Conference both significant in itself as an event and also historically very interesting from the point of the view of the direction and future of the Anglican Communion. One the one hand, the last three conferences have established modes of preparation and program that have changed the perception of their role in the life of the Anglican Communion and given the resolutions of the conferences a new profile. At the same time, conflicts over the place of homosexuality in the public life of the church have been engulfing the new institutions in the Anglican Communion.

Clearly there have been conflicts before. The first Lambeth Conference in 1867 was finally pressed for out of concerns for the institutional arrangements in the colonial churches and their capacity to deal with doctrinal conflicts such as those recently experienced in Southern Africa. The bishop of Natal, J. W. Colenso, had been deposed by the bishop of Cape Town after a tribunal condemned his writings. The Privy Council ruled that there was no legal basis for this act, and Colenso stayed in his position with the help of funds from England. These events alarmed a number of colonial bishops who thought it undermined their own situation and pressed the Archbishop of Canterbury to call a conference to deal with this situation. The question was how perceived heresy could be dealt with in the institutional arrangements that existed at that time in the provinces of worldwide Anglicanism.

However, it should not be overlooked that there had been moves from the U.S. for an Anglican Council, and Bishop Gray had been advocating an imperial synod well before his troubles with Colenso. This imperial synod would not have included the American bishops, and some of the earlier suggestions from Canada and in England make the same assumption. The "synod" was to be an aspect of the bonds encompassed by the empire. At the first conference, there was continuing debate about a synodical structure, but in the end a pan-Anglican Congress emerged, which happened eventually in 1908, and the episcopal conferences moved eventually in the direction of a consultative conference.[1]

There are many similarities between the situation in the 1860s and what has emerged in the last decade. In the present situation, mainly African bishops want action taken against two other Anglican provinces because they have acted in ways they perceive to be heretical. Like their ex-patriot colonial episcopal predecessors, they want some kind of global action taken to discipline heretical actions taken by two provinces. They complain that the instruments of the Anglican Communion have not exercised any authority to enforce the resolution on this subject passed at the 1998 Lambeth Conference. In the Colenso case, the colonial bishops wanted the power to deal with the heretical bishop to lie with the local province and were looking for wider support for that provincial authority. The Windsor Process and the pursuit of a covenant are precisely attempts to change the institutional arrangements in the Anglican Communion in order to deal with the conflict over the place of homosexuality in the public life of the church. The power being sought is to deal with a province, not a bishop.

There have been earlier conflicts over issues of sexual ethics such as marriage and divorce practices. There are some similarities between the arguments over polygamy and homosexuality. Both arise in the context of the interaction between gospel and culture. Both have to do with how what is perceived to be a gospel truth of universal application can be applied in a cultural context where the pattern of social life in different. This is the point rightly identified by Peter Akinola in relation to homosexuality when he announced GAFCON.

The Lambeth Conference first addressed the issue of polygamy in 1888, when a strict exclusion policy was adopted. People in polygamous relations could not be baptized and were to "be kept under Christian instruction until such time as they shall be in a position to accept the law of Christ."[2] A report was called for in 1920 and a serious problem acknowl-

1. See Stephenson, *First Lambeth Conference*, and also the reflections on the similarities of the first and the current conferences in Stevenson, *Fallible Church*.

2. LC 1888, 5.

edged and not yet solved was admitted in 1958. In 1968 the conference recognized that polygamy posed "one of the sharpest conflicts between the faith and particular cultures." But it asserted its commitment to monogamous life-long marriage as God's will for mankind."[3] It was not until the 1988 Lambeth Conference that some kind of resolution was agreed upon. Monogamy was upheld as the ideal relationship of love between husband and wife; nevertheless, a polygamist convert may be baptized and confirmed with his wives and children on the conditions that he does not marry again while any of his wives are alive, that the local Anglican community agrees to his acceptance, and that he would not be compelled to put away his wives on account of the social deprivation they would suffer. Provinces were encouraged to share information about how they handle these situations pastorally. Here you have a moderation of a general principle because its operation in the local context produces harm. It is a modus operandi. This challenge, as with marriage and divorce, has turned on the relation of the gospel to the cultural context.

But the place of homosexuality in the public life of the church has been treated differently and has led to actions that directly challenge traditional institutional relations between provinces. Some bishops and primates have ordained priests and bishops to work in other people's dioceses. Primates have sought to make demands about the internal operation of provinces, and the so-called Instruments of Unity have been challenged. Their advice has been rejected and their warnings snubbed. Some Primates have used symbolic gestures to make clear their objections, such as refusing to take communion with other primates or with the Archbishop of Canterbury. The Lambeth Conference has also been subjected to this kind of symbolic action with some bishops announcing they will not go to Lambeth.

Recent Lambeth Conferences have attracted a range of "preparatory" events where similarly minded bishops and others met to talk about the issues they thought would arise at the conference. In 2008 that pattern continued, but it was overshadowed by a much larger conference called by four African primates, the primate of the Southern Cone in South America and the Archbishop of Sydney. In January 2007, Peter Akinola, the Primate of the Church of Nigeria (Anglican Communion), announced that there would be a conference in Jerusalem in June 2008 called a Global Anglican

3. LC 1968, 23.

Future Conference (GAFCON). He declared that the conference was called by "those members of the Anglican Family who see themselves as orthodox Anglicans, who are upholding the authority of scriptures, and believe that the time has come to come together to fashion the future of our Anglican family." These he set over against those who were allowing "modern culture to overwhelm the word of God" and interpreting the Bible "in a way that suits their fancy" and "giving prominence to modern culture."

In a contrast which set the tone for the public perception of this conference he went on to say "Those of us who will abide with the Word of God, come rain come fire, are those who are in GAFCON. Those who say it does not matter are the ones who are attending Lambeth" . . . "Uganda, Rwanda, Sydney, Nigeria: we are not going to Lambeth conference. What is the use of the Lambeth conference for a three weeks jamboree which will sweep these issues under the carpet. GAFCON will confer about the future of the church, which will set a road map for the future."[4]

These enthusiastic words came to be modified in the publicity of the conference and a number of bishops announced that they would be going to both Lambeth and GAFCON. In later publicity GAFCON, transformed itself into a pilgrimage to the biblical lands and denied it was an alternative to Lambeth. "The pilgrimage is to strengthen bishops at a crucial time in the life of the Anglican Communion. Many bishops will not be able to accept the invitation to the Lambeth Conference as their consciences will not allow it. Some will attend both gatherings. The purpose of the consultation is to strengthen them all spiritually." Nonetheless the emphasis on a broadly evangelistic agenda and growth was very apparent.

> Our pastoral responsibility to the people we lead is now to provide the opportunity to come together around the central and unchanging tenets of the central and unchanging historic Anglican faith. Rather than being subject to the continued chaos and compromise that have dramatically impeded Anglican mission, GAFCON will seek to clarify this call at this time and build a network of cooperation for Global mission. Communion depends on having something in common. Churches in the Global South are growing. They're passionate about the truth and their faith. We are building on this strength.[5]

4. Quotes taken from http://www.gafcon.org. It is interesting that there is no reference here to Kenya, Tanzania or the Southern Cone.

5. This material was accessed on May 12, 2008 from http://www.gafcon.org/index.php?option=com_content&task=view&id=4&Itemid=4. A check in June 2009 revealed that

This is clearly a conference for churches that see themselves as growing churches and are committed to what they see as the unchanging gospel of christian faith. It is the second half of this claim that presumably prompts them to claim the title orthodox.

It is not at all clear how this conference relates to the Global South Network, which had come into being as a result of a conference of mission agencies in 1986 in order to facilitate and encourage mission in appropriate terms in the Global South countries. Churches in Asia and Oceania were included in this network, but they are entirely absent from the leadership of GAFCON, and a significant number of their bishops seem to have been absent from the conference itself. Given some criticism of the conference from Asia, perhaps they were not invited.

The conference leaders have consistently claimed that the issue is not just homosexuality, it is about authority. They complain about a lack of authority in the Communion to control the North American churches, and they speak of the underlying authority of the Bible, which they say is compromised or dismissed by the North American revisionists. In his initial press statement, Peter Akinola declared that the difference was between those who accepted the authority of the Bible no matter what, and those who gave prominence to culture and interpret the Bible to suit their fancy. This really touches on the substantial issue. Not the authority of the Bible of itself, but how its authority works in relation to the culture in which the Christian is called to be faithful. That is not just a question of the way particular texts are interpreted either in relation to other texts or the originating context; it also has to do with the kind of authority Scripture exercises in relation to assumptions of the cultural context in which it is read and its relation to other factors and warrants in decision-making. These questions touch on quite substantial issues of epistemology and theological method. To exclude their consideration from the debate as if it were just a matter of interpretation pre-judges important and decisive questions.

On the precise issue of sexuality, the GAFCON speakers have accused the North Americans of giving in to culture and thus accepting the rights of gay and lesbian people into the public life of the church. It is true that the issue of sexuality in The Episcopal Church arose in connection with cultural movements to do with civil rights in the broader

this material has been deleted from the GAFCON website, presumably when it was reconstructed after the conference

U.S. culture. That was also true earlier in North America in relation to the place of women, their membership of the General Convention of the church, and their ordination as priests and bishops. It was relatively recently, in 1967, that the Sexual Offences Acts in the United Kingdom decriminalized homosexual acts in private. The then-Archbishop of Canterbury, Dr. Geoffrey Fisher, supported the bill on the grounds that the law should not intrude into the private arena. Only in 2007 did the UK parliament pass a law allowing for civil recognition of same-sex relationships. Clearly in Western countries the tide of human rights is running strongly.[6]

But this precise issue of homosexuality in the wider culture arises also in Africa. In Nigeria, Uganda, Kenya, and Tanzania homosexual acts are forbidden by law and subject to criminal sanctions.[7] Furthermore, in Nigeria in 2006 laws to forbid blessing same-sex relationships and any promotion of homosexual activity were actively supported by Peter Akinola and the Nigerian church in the following terms: "The Church commends the law-makers for their prompt reaction to outlaw same-sex relationships in Nigeria and calls for the bill to be passed since the idea expressed in the bill is the moral position of Nigerians regarding human sexuality."[8]

The Primates of Nigeria, Uganda, Kenya, and Tanzania have been the core leadership of GAFCON, and they support the culture of their own countries in opposition to homosexuality. The congruence between the cultural norms and the preferred biblical interpretation in both North America and in these African countries raises a difficult question for the terms of this argument as set out by Peter Akinola. Clearly Christians are called to live their lives in the terms of the Kingdom of God, a kingdom that is not of this world. But that does not mean that Christians are called always to be in opposition to the world around them. The New Testament narrates the struggle to see what is significant in the new Christian truth that is personal and universal in its reach in a way that both fulfills and transforms the Old Testament revelation.

6. See Charlesworth, *Writing in Rights*, and Hegarty and Leonard, *Human Rights*.

7. Radner and Goddard, "Human Rights, Homosexuality and the Anglican Communion." For a general overview of laws in relation to homosexuality, see Ottosson, "State-Sponsored Homophobia."

8. Church of Nigeria, "Message to the Nation/Communiqué."

Peter Akinola correctly puts his finger on the crux issue of the cultural context of biblical authority. How is the Bible to be interpreted in relation to the host culture so that Christians can be faithful to their gospel vocation? The issue of the authority of the Bible is inevitably and quite properly worked out in the context of seeking to be faithful in the terms of the culture and circumstances in which God has called you. The issue here is not, Do you accept the authority of the Bible? Rather it is, How do you use the Bible in your context in a way that is faithful to its authority in Anglican Christianity and to the witness you are called to render where you are? It is an argument about contextualization. That process can be seen at work on almost every page of the New Testament. It is not simply a matter of rejecting the cultural context and asserting the authority of the Bible, as if it stood separate in the way that Peter Akinola declares.

The reality is that the very process of reading Scripture is conducted in a cultural context with tacit assumptions that will in varying degrees be different from those of the authors of the texts. Handling that difference is part of the challenge of faithful interpretation. Moreover, understanding Scripture in the service of faithful witness to Christ in specific cultural and social circumstances brings into play wider theological considerations. These issues do not diminish the authority of Scripture; they simply characterize the operation of the authority of Scripture. Defining the question in terms of dualistic absolutes is in fact seriously to diminish the authority of Scripture and to ignore the patterns manifest in the New Testament.

## Global Anglican Future Conference (GAFCON)

From June 22–29, 2008, about a thousand people met in Jerusalem for GAFCON. Like most international conferences, it brought together people from a wide variety of backgrounds and cultures that fostered enthusiasm and inspiration. At the end of the conference, a three part Final Statement was agreed upon; a statement on the global Anglican context, a creedal-like Jerusalem Declaration, and a section looking to the future.[9] The conference declared that GAFCON was not just a conference but a movement, and that it had a future. It set out its mission in the context of a picture of the corruption of the churches in the Western world by the forces of secularism and pluralism. There is an extraordinary confidence

9. The statement is available online under the title "The Jerusalem Declaration" at the Fellowship of Confessing Anglicans website: http://fca.net/decstat.html.

in the language of this text. It sets out what it claims are "undeniable facts concerning world Anglicanism."

> The first fact is the acceptance and promotion within the provinces of the Anglican Communion of a different "gospel" (cf. Galatians 1:6–8) which is contrary to the apostolic gospel. . . .
> The second fact is the declaration by provincial bodies in the Global South that they are out of communion with bishops and churches that promote this false gospel. . . .
> The third fact is the manifest failure of the Communion Instruments to exercise discipline in the face of overt heterodoxy. We can only come to the devastating conclusion that "we are a global Communion with a colonial structure."

The first is not a fact at all. It is a claim from one side of an ongoing argument. The second is true but potentially misleading in that not all provinces in the Global South have said these things. Whether they are wise, sensible, or adequate things to be said might be another matter. The third is yet again a claim from one of a number of sides in an ongoing argument. These are not facts; they are assertions that are widely known to be controverted and known to be controverted by the GAFCON organizers. This "undeniable fact" language is really a form of rhetoric. The extreme form of expression makes it difficult to regard these claims as serious contributions to any kind of conversation among Anglicans worldwide. And that presumably is an indication of the direction of this movement. It is going its own way.

The second statement refers to cross-border episcopal appointments and concludes that "a major realignment has occurred and will continue to unfold." Of course these actions were taken in defiance of the authority of the Instruments of the Anglican Communion that they complain has not been enforced against others. The former metropolitan nations that had sent missionaries and bishops will now be the recipients of bishops sent from former dependencies. The former periphery will now be the metropolitan center, and the former metropolitan center will be the new periphery. The third statement about the failure of the metropolitan-dominated Anglican Communion to discipline its own members leads to the conclusion that this is truly the old colonialism.

This reference to being a "global communion with a colonial structure" is in quotation marks and presumably has been retained here in abbreviated form from a previous edition of the statement. But it is all the more revealing as bringing to the surface some of the underlying cultural and political impulses at play in this controversy. The major realignment is not simply about sending bishops and clergy. It is about a whole new view of the world that involves a reversal of the old metropolitan–periphery pattern. This is the language of postcolonialism, and it is not surprising that an African-inspired movement should reflect thinking and emotions that are to be found in the wider postcolonial world and literature.[10] This is residual anti-colonial sentiment in the dynamics of Global South political life and is part of the cultural context within which Anglicans seek to fulfill their Christian vocation. Even someone living in an "old empire" country like Australia can feel some sympathy for these feelings from Africa.

This is an important dynamic in this movement and should be recognized both as a force in this turmoil and also for what it actually is. Worldwide Anglicanism has been affected by a number of "empires." The Japanese empire and Anglican mission in Korea, the twentieth-century Australian colonial mandate and Anglican mission in Papua New Guinea, most significantly the British Empire in its eighteenth-, nineteenth-, and twentieth-century colonies, and the U.S. empire and missions to the Philippines, countries in Latin America and Taiwan. The U.S. fought a war of independence, and Anglicans were forced into separate independence from Britain and into close relationship with the new republic. Canada, South Africa, New Zealand, and Australia gained local representative government during the nineteenth century, and many colonies in Africa gained their independence in the second half of the twentieth century. The Episcopal Church in the U.S. has incorporated the churches of the more informal but still powerful empire of the U.S. into its metropolitan membership.

All these imperial/colonial relationships carried some questionable attitudes and habits of thought for people on both sides. We may rightly wish to go beyond colonial and imperial Anglicanism, but we should not underestimate the power of the underlying sentiments that different people and groups bring to that challenge. Achieving the mentality that is appropriate to relations within worldwide Anglicanism is not something likely to be achieved in a single generation.

10. See Sanneh, *Encountering the West* and *Whose Religion Is Christianity?*; Ndungane, "Scripture"; and Douglas and Pui-Lan, *Beyond Colonial Anglicanism*.

Once again we are confronted with the issue of the relation between cultural forces and the formulation of Christian vocation. It is hard to imagine how sending missionaries from one place to another in appropriate circumstances could be a bad thing. Exercising control through differences in power between parts of the church is a quite different matter, and it is presumably what this document and its authors are addressing. Of course, the corruption of ecclesial mutuality by one party (the old empire) does not justify returning the compliment being returned by others (the new empire). It might be understandable, and it might not be easy for the former imperial center to make that point. But the point needs to be made nonetheless. The church is called to a mutuality that is not corrupted by cultural forces, and such a vocation ought to engender humility about our pasts and in our current actions. These are not new struggles in the church. They are found quite precisely in Paul's dealings with the Corinthians, in Jesus' teaching to his contemporaries, and in the struggles of the apostles to embrace the mission to the gentiles.

The Jerusalem declaration of faith makes numerous gestures to the Anglican Reformation heritage: the allusion to the language of the 1603 canons for the expression of the doctrinal foundations of Anglican identity, and the references to the 1662 Book of Common Prayer, its ordinal, and the Thirty-Nine Articles of Religion. The appeal to the first four councils is also an Anglican note, though there seems to be little sense of the pre-Reformation Anglican heritage or of the highly centralized political and constitutional revolution that effected the institutional changes of the English reformation. Are we to understand that GAFCON embraces the Royal Supremacy as affirmed in Article 37? These documents do not escape their historical context simply by being quoted.

This section of the statement concludes the negative view of the Anglican Communion in its present form. The Anglican Communion is so damaged "that it cannot simply be patched back together." GAFCON claims to be a fellowship of confessing Anglicans, a fellowship that includes "provinces, dioceses, churches, missionary jurisdictions, parachurch organizations and individual Anglican Christians." Their goal is to reform, and they are not breaking away. The document asserts its confessional identity in fairly traditional terms, but then declares "we do not accept that Anglican identity is determined necessarily through recognition by the Archbishop of Canterbury." This is a crucial issue for GAFCON, and it is not surprising that the standing of the Archbishop of Canterbury has been under attack. The Primate of Uganda, Henry Orombi, did so on the grounds that the archbishop is appointed by a secular government.[11] But hardly any provincial constitution in worldwide Anglicanism suggests that Anglican identity for any province or diocese is settled by recognition by the Archbishop of Canterbury. George Carey said he did not recognize the consecration of American bishops in Africa for work in the U.S., but this was for procedural reasons to do with the current constitutions of the provinces involved. In any case many provincial constitutions establish communion with the Church of England, not the Archbishop of Canterbury. Fellowship with the Church of England was the basis for invitations to the first Lambeth Conference. Some provincial constitutions provide that if the Church of England departs from the faith as set out in their constitution then they might terminate their communion with the Church of England. Nonetheless one can sympathize with the identity issue that GAFCON has created for itself, even if it is construed in historically mistaken terms.

Clause 8 of the GAFCON declaration affirms a view of marriage as the framework for the stance on homosexuality. The reference to freedom on secondary matters in clause 12 points to a key issue in this project. The border between core and non-core matters is being clarified. In sharp contrast to the Righter judgment in ECUSA,[12] which declared that teaching on homosexuality was not part of the core teaching of the church, the Jerusalem declaration clearly takes the view not only against homosexuality but also that such a view is clearly part of the core teachings of the gospel. Acceptance of this practice by the church represents another false gospel. This is argued on the basis that it is a key moral question about the nature of the family.

The language of conscience in this document and in earlier justifications of these actions covers a prior step. A matter does not become a matter of conscience simply by asserting it to be so. A judgment about the rightness or otherwise of such an action cannot be separated from the question of conscience. It only becomes a matter of conscience when a judgment has been made that the action is right or wrong. But that matter

11. See *The Times* newspaper of London, August 1, 2008. "The Church cannot heal this crisis of betrayal." http://www.timesonline.co.uk/tol/comment/columnists/guest_contributors/article4438729.ece

12. For more on the Righter judgment, see: http://www.episcopalchurch.org/19625_12931_ENG_HTM.htm.

of judgment is precisely a point in dispute, and to eclipse it by rushing to the language of conscience is less than adequate.

The tradition of territorial episcopal jurisdiction is clearly secondary in this document, since its observation cannot stand in the way of gospel truth. This is something of an oddity in that some of the primates and bishops involved in these operations have subscribed oaths of office in church constitutions that make this territorial arrangement a clear commitment. So we have the unhappy sight of bishops who on oath are committed to observing this territorial jurisdiction at the same time breaking that rule in other places. The issue then becomes not just a matter of legal detail, but the honesty of those bishops. Given the kinds of institutional arrangements within which Anglicans work, the distinction between order and morality is not as easily sustained as some seem to think.

The tone and assumptions of the text are disappointing. It is clearly staking out territory to provide a basis for the development of future networks and organizational jurisdictions. In this context it is a form of doublespeak to claim that they are not leaving the Anglican Communion. The issue is not so much that they are setting out away from the current Anglican Communion organizational arrangements; the real problem is that this document and presumably this movement have set their sail not to engage with those with whom they say they so fundamentally disagree. Such actions create difficulties for future bridge building by entrenching current disputes in organizational forms. That is a more serious matter and a worrying failure.

## Lambeth Conference

The 2008 Lambeth conference was the thirteenth in the series and the fourth in the modern residential style of gathering. The first eight conferences were held at Lambeth Palace. The ninth conference in 1968 was hailed as a new-look conference. It was held in Church House in London, and for the first time media representatives were allowed into some sessions. The novelty of the conference was created not just by the different location and program, but also by the exciting times in which it took place. The 1958 conference had been preceded by the Pan-Anglican Congress at Minneapolis in 1954. It was a time for expansive visions on a global scale, and the new Executive Officer of the Anglican Communion was appointed in the year following the Lambeth Conference. The 1968 Lambeth

Conference followed the 1961 New Delhi Assembly of the World Council of Churches, which was addressed by the new Archbishop of Canterbury, Michael Ramsey. This great ecumenical gathering was followed in 1962 by the opening of the great renovating, or so it seemed at the time, Second Vatican Council.

Anglicans were caught up in these movements and the Pan-Anglican Congress at Toronto followed in 1963, which left on the table the enthusiastic document Mutual Responsibility and Interdependence (MRI) in the Body of Christ. Coming out of North American energy and national confidence, it challenged the Anglican Communion to be more coherent and corporate. The Congress stimulated numerous books on global Anglicanism, and the program for the congress reflected this confident outward-looking mood. The theme was "The Church's Mission to the World," which was carried forward under titles that placed the church on frontiers of various kinds. Not only did it reflect American leadership in the Communion, it also served to reinforce the dynamism running in Western societies of the new decade of the 1960s. MRI became something of a focus for these forces in various parts of the Anglican Communion.

Despite this American dynamism, relations at the Lambeth Conference were still moderated. The assessment of bishop Luxton of Huron in Canada reflected approvingly that the American bishops were more comfortable in the debates than in 1958 and took a large part in the conference. "And their English brethren seem on the whole to have accepted them almost as equals."[13]

This new-style Lambeth Conference of 1968 set the tone for subsequent conferences in the second half of the twentieth century. In 1968 there were thirty-three committees in the conference gathered under three themes. Preparatory papers had been published and twenty-six consultants participated in the conference to facilitate the debates. Seventy-six observers attended, and the global organization grew by the establishment of the Anglican Consultative Council with bishops, clergy, and laity from each province. The report on Inter-Anglican Structure envisaged the Worldwide Congresses being replaced by joint meetings of the Anglican representatives at the WCC assemblies and the ACC to be held at the time of the WCC assemblies.

---

13. Stephenson, *Anglicanism and the Lambeth Conferences*, 257.

The enthusiasm of the 1960s had dimmed by 1978, though the conference continued to grow in size, especially with bishops from Africa. The statistics provided in the book of preparatory information showed clearly that membership of Anglican churches was falling in Western countries and growing in Africa. The conference moved from London to the campus of the University of Kent in Canterbury and lasted three weeks. A similar program structure pertained with small groups, Bible studies, and plenary hearings. There were only twenty consultants, nine of whom came from England. The conference passed only thirty-seven resolutions, the lowest number since 1888.[14]

However a new transition was under way. While in 1968 the American bishops were beginning to feel more accepted, by 1978 the consequences of the "winds of change" blowing through the British Empire and Commonwealth were appearing on the horizon like a cloud the size of a man's hand. The decolonization agenda of British Prime Minister Harold MacMillan and the drive to establish independent Anglican Provinces promoted by archbishop Geoffrey Fisher were beginning to have consequences in the membership and balance of the Lambeth Conference.

The 1988 conference report declared that the twelfth conference was not only the largest ever held—518 compared with 76 at the first conference—but also perhaps the best prepared.[15] Perhaps this confidence reflects the extensive regional meetings held around the Communion to identify issues that were then taken up in preparatory studies, which were in turn incorporated into the St. Augustine's seminar that then produced the working papers for the conference. There were the usual elements in the conference program, with four main sections from which seventy-three resolutions were agreed in plenary sessions. These were published along with the section reports.

The 1998 Lambeth conference continued these trends. It was bigger than ever with 750 bishops and had the same regional meetings to identify concerns. These in turn were processed through a seminar and preparatory papers were provided to the bishops. Plenary sessions considered

---

14. The resolutions passed at each conference have been: 1878–12, 1888–19, 1897–63, 1908–78, 1920–80, 1930–75, 1948–118, 1958–131, 1968–69, 1978–37, 1988–73, 1998–94. The resolutions in later conferences have also tended to be longer and more complex.

15. Lambeth Conference, *Truth Shall Make You Free*, 1.

resolutions that had been developed out of the discussion in the meetings of the four thematic sections. This resulted in ninety-four resolutions.

There has been a gathering momentum in the last three Lambeth Conferences giving priority to preparation for the conference in terms of what are perceived to be the critical issues in provinces around the globe. These are then streamed through to a process that produced resolutions on these matters. The expectation in this process is that the Lambeth Conference will address the problems of the Communion. It has the effect of encouraging the idea that the conference has some of the marks of a parliament or synod and that its resolutions as a consequence should be regarded as procedurally authoritative. The reporting by the world media encouraged this understanding as they presented the conference as a kind of summit of Anglicanism.

At the 1998 conference there was intense and heated argument at the final plenary session when a resolution on homosexuality was debated and amended. In the full glare of the mass media, deep divisions were on display. That intensity arose not just because those involved thought the subject was very important, it was also because they thought that a resolution at the Lambeth Conference meant that something would happen as a result. That is exactly how the GAFCON primates interpret the conference and this resolution. They complain it has not been enforced.

The introduction to the official report of the 1998 conference declared that the bishops met to worship and pray and to talk and study the Bible together. Undoubtedly, the bishops who attended mostly experienced these things at the conference. But the public reality and the rhetorical reality subsequently placed on the resolutions by some bishops and primates have been significantly different. Clearly this pattern of conference was not developing in a way that simply engendered personal exchanges, worship and talk. It was beginning to look more like a conference to make declarations and lay down definitions on points of doctrine and other matters; exactly the opposite of what Archbishop Longley envisaged when he called the first conference, and which subsequent conferences have consistently asserted to be the purpose. So the 2008 Lambeth Conference presented a very significant challenge for those planning it, especially the archbishop of Canterbury, Rowan Williams.

Rowan Williams made his thoughts known well in advance when he wrote to the Primates in March 2006. The 1998 resolution on sexuality would not be re-visited, though there would be space to reflect on the work being done in the Provinces on this subject and also time to think about the theological principles and practical suggestions made in the Windsor Report. But the main focus would be "equipping the people of God." He was looking for a style of meeting that could maximize opportunities for training and development. There would be no large section groups, but smaller groups for discussion. At this stage he anticipated plenary sessions and resolutions, though with the caveat that there needed to be processes in place that would enable people to know that any resolutions have had an effect.[16]

In the letter of invitation to bishops in May 2007, there was no mention of resolutions but an emphasis on the interactive style of conference being planned. It would focus on shared experience of God, renewal for effective ministry, and be a place where

> we can get more clarity about the limits of our diversity and the means of deepening our Communion. It is an occasion when the Archbishop of Canterbury exercises his privilege of calling his colleagues together, not to legislate but to discover and define something more about our common identity through prayer, listening to God's Word and shared reflection. It is an occasion to rediscover the reality of the Church itself as a worldwide community united by the call and grace of Christ.[17]

It is not a council or synod of bishops he declared and has no constitution or formal powers. Nonetheless he says that the "Instruments of Communion" have provided a set of resources focused on the Windsor Report and covenant proposals, and he makes it clear that he hopes that acceptance of the invitation will carry with it a willingness to work with the Windsor process and the covenant proposals.[18]

The actual program turned out to be strikingly different from the previous three conferences. The whole conference began with a three day retreat and ended with just two days when there was plenary debate. Each day there were the usual small group Bible studies and plenary worship. Instead of large sections working on broad themes and producing a report from which resolutions were developed, there were relatively small "indaba" groups in which bishops were able to listen to each other and

16. See Anglican Communion News Service, "Archbishop sets out thinking."

17. See the press release about the letter at: www.archbishopofcanterbury.org/469.

18. See Anglican Communion News Service, "First invitations."

discuss matters that were important to them. There were also self-select group meetings and a marketplace where presentations were available and a number of "hearings" sessions during the conference from the Windsor Working Group and the Covenant Design Group. At the end of the conference, a document of reflections from the conversations in the indaba groups was presented to the conference, and members were asked in the drafting process not, did they agree with it? but, did they hear their voice in the document, along of course with many other voices? The status of the document was described by Chair of the Reflections Group as "narrative." It is an attempt to capture something of the conversations that took place in the indaba or listening groups.[19]

Rowan Williams placed his stamp on the conference not just in his influence on the shape of the program, but also through his retreat addresses and through three presidential addresses given during the course of the conference. The first address at the beginning of the conference after the retreat set the bishops meeting in the context of God's own action and their life in the presence of God. What matters most is that "God's eyes are upon us and that God has entrusted something to us." He rejected the notion that the new style of conference substitutes process for substance. Anyway many of the resolutions of the past were never acted upon. Furthermore these previous methods were "very much tied to Western ways—and not only Western ways, but the habits that developed in the later twentieth century." Often the voices that were heard were those most used to working those sorts of procedures.

This conference would try to allow all voices to be heard so that there is some clarity about what the questions really are and at least some degree of shared perspective on things. What he therefore hopes for at the end of the conference is a "'Reflection' from the conference that is not a set of resolutions and decisions, but which does genuinely change the situation and take us forward." In some strong language he declared that the greatest need for the Communion at the present time was for "transformed relationships. Habits of respect, patience and understanding that are fleshed out in specific ways and changed habits."

He rejected the idea of the Anglican Communion as a loose federation with diverse parts operating side by side in competition, or a family

19. Details of the conference can be found on the Lambeth Conference web site http://www.lambethconference.org/index.cfm from which the texts of Rowan Williams' addresses to the conference and the Reflections document are quoted in this chapter.

of regional national churches strictly demarcated from each other and coming together from time to time or in terms of a firmer and more consistent control of diversity. His fourth way is that of council and covenant, where covenant represents an intensification of relationship for those who want it, rather than as an instrument of exclusion. A covenant is essential in order to give such a vision clearer definition.

In his second presidential address he returned to these themes and set out what he imagined might at this point in the conference people hoped had been heard by those who disagreed with them. What might, for example, the traditionalist hope others have heard? It underlined the strong theme in the conference for Williams that all should be heard and that they should have some confidence that they had been heard fairly.

That character of the conference can be seen through various windows. The first window is the Reflections document that gave a "narrative" of the conversations in the indaba groups. This is a long document with thirteen sections gathered together in two groups under the headings of the two stated aims of the conference. "Equipping Bishops for God's Mission" reports on missions and evangelism, human and social justice, environment, ecumenism, and relations with other religions. In general terms these are the sorts of topics that have been the concern of earlier conferences. "Strengthening Anglican Identity" reports on bishops and Anglican identity, human sexuality, the Scriptures, an Anglican Covenant, the Windsor Process, and statements of solidarity with those who have presented their concerns to the conference. These are clearly the issues of 2008; not surprisingly the document reports a variety of opinions. There are twelve different ways of proceeding on sexuality, and also twelve concerns listed about the St. Andrew's draft of the covenant and ten practical suggestions listed for the Covenant Design Group. This document is extremely useful as an *aide memoir* of conversations. It will disappoint some because it does not contain resolutions, let alone decisions. But it certainly gives some sense of the kinds of things discussed in the small groups.

The Bible studies have always been central to modern Lambeth Conferences. They tap into a fundamental commitment to Scripture reading and to the vitality that comes from encounters with fellow Christians living in different cultures and situations. The self-select groups and their presentations or contributions have not become available to the wider public, and only a summary of the contribution of the Windsor Continuation Group's presentation to its hearings is available. There was a gathering organized by Global South bishops that a considerable number attended. Ten bishops from the Global South issued a statement of their position. They affirmed the growth and value of the Global South network; they urged the immediate implementation of the proposals for a Pastoral Forum and for the Lambeth conference to affirm the Windsor developments and the moratoria. They also expressed concern "with the continuing patronizing attitude of the West towards the rest of the churches worldwide."[20] Others, of course, made press statements and declarations and even Gene Robinson was reported to have been seen around the campus of the university from time to time.

In the final presidential address, Williams set himself the task of trying to articulate not just what the message of Lambeth 2008 might be but also what was the place from which the bishops might speak. He began by noting the strong desire expressed at the conference not to separate, and he noted with thanks that the bishops at the conference had taken responsibility for each other. But that only raised the question, What is the unity that is apparently sought so much? Here, Williams takes a strongly christological step in his argument.

> We are one with one another because we are called into union with the one Christ and stand in his unique place—stand *in* the Way, the Truth and the Life. Our unity is not mutual forbearance but being summoned and drawn into the same place before the Father's throne. *That* unity is a pure gift—and something we can think of in fear and trembling as well as wordless gratitude; because to be in that place is to be in the light of absolute Truth, naked and defenseless.

Such unity is inseparable from truth and is broken not by disagreement but when "we stop being able to see in each other the same kind of conviction of being called by an authoritative voice into a place where none of us has an automatic right to stand."

The next step in the argument was to show that Christians express their unity in a number of visible, tangible ways, Bible reading and living by what they read and consistent practices around the sacraments of baptism and Eucharist. The commonality of these practices enables us to see each other as standing in the same Way and the same Truth. All Christian groups and associations do this, that is to say they make "some

---

20. See "Our Statement as Global South Primates at Lambeth, para 8." Online: episcopalegypt.blogspot.com/2008/08/i-signed-this-statement-from-global.html.

sort of 'covenant' for the sake of mutual recognition, mutual gratitude and mutual learning." Williams then applies this to the current difficulties and argues that new things need some space for conversation and testing, but that patience is confused when it is claimed that the new thing carries the "Church's authority." That, he suggests is the background to the pleas of moratoria both for church practices in relation to homosexuals and also interventions across provinces by bishops. In regard to interventions, he makes the point that such actions carry the unlikely implication that there is nothing by way of pastoral oversight that can be offered by the incumbent bishop. He encourages the development of covenants in terms of mutual agreements between bishops about a personal "rule of life." In one of the important steps in the argument, he argues that a covenant

> has the potential to make us more of a church; more of a "catholic" church in the proper sense, a church, that is, which understands its ministry and service and sacraments as united and interdependent throughout the world. That we wanted to move in such a direction would in itself be a weighty message. But it might even be a prophetic one. The vision of a global Church of interdependent communities is not the vision of an ecclesiastical world empire— or even a colonial relic. . . . The global horizon of the Church matters because churches without this are always in danger of slowly surrendering to the culture around them and losing sight of their calling to challenge that culture.

He cites the Church of England as historically so involved in the political structures that it often had little to say that was properly critical, and he praises the faithful Christians in Zimbabwe whose stand in the face of corruption was assisted by belonging to a wider fellowship of the Anglican Communion. This is a very significant shift in the terms for understanding the Communion and its problems. The turn to catholicity opens up a more creative diversity and also a better sense of continuity, tradition, and faithfulness than the idea of unity that especially in its modern context carries within its semantic range many obstacles to a genuinely Anglican ecclesiology. Catholicity is not without its problems, but it is a more fruitful way of approaching these issues. This reference to catholicity leads Williams to his summary peroration.

> This is the Catholic Church; this is the Catholic faith—a global vision for a global wound, a global claim on our service. None of it is intelligible without belief in the one divine Saviour, raised from

the dead, pouring out the gifts of his Spirit. To our Communion many gifts have been given, and God wills to give many more if we let him. In these days together we have not overcome our problems or reinvented our structures: that will still take time. We have quite a strong degree of support for a Pastoral Forum to support minorities, a strong consensus on the need to examine how the Instruments of Communion will best work, and a recognition—though still with many questions—that a Covenant is needed. We have a strongly expressed intention to place our international development work on a firmer and more co-ordinated footing.

Rowan Williams followed the conference with a pastoral letter to all the bishops in the Anglican Communion in which he set out his perspectives as to where the conference had been led.[21] He traversed much of the ground of his final address, though in slightly stronger terms in relation to the nature of the conference as consultative and listening. He claimed that the covenant would help to shape and confirm identity for the Anglican Communion and thus build cohesion, though he notes that the bishops wanted to avoid a legalistic of juridical tone in the covenant document. He takes the reflections document as containing pointers to where common goals and assumptions are in the Communion. When he gets to development work, he speaks of agreement among the bishops that this work needs to more coordinated. He looks to the possibility of using the indaba methods in meetings of the Primates and the ACC, and he refers to the contribution of the guest speakers who challenged the bishops on the integration of social passion with theology and the nature of the unity sought within the Anglican Communion and with other churches. While there are a few refinements in this letter, it essentially draws into focus what he had said at the conference. It has the effect of placing on the record in a succinct form Williams' view of the conference.

Lambeth 2008 was clearly directed by an overriding vision from Rowan Williams. It was a radically different kind of conference, and it aimed for a radically different kind of influence on worldwide Anglicans. The clearest contrast is with the form of the conference as compared with the three that preceded it. The pre-conference preparation in those conferences identified critical issues in the Communion and these were processed through the conference structure to produce resolutions. There had been resolutions from earlier conferences, but they had been resolu-

---

21. The text is available at http://aco.org/acns/news.cfm/2008/8/26/ACNS4514.

tions to give expression to the opinions of the bishops on a variety of topics. In the last three conferences, the very character of the conference made the resolutions look much more like decisions of some kind, whether they were decisions that implied some kind of action or some point of view that should somehow be taken as institutionally authoritative in the Anglican Communion. Lambeth 2008 completely broke that trend by the very character of the program of the conference. Instead of organizationally authoritative resolutions, there were no resolutions at all.

There were, however, some curious absences at this conference. Given the thrust of the Reflections document, where was the affirmation and contribution of theology here? There is scant reference to the work of TEAC, which was designated in the preliminary material as having a significant role to play in the conference and in the renewal of Anglican faith around the Communion, especially in the area of Anglican identity. There is hardly any reference to the latest Inter-Anglican Theological and Doctrinal Commission report, *Conflict and Hope*, which was published in February 2008, and which dealt directly with issues of conflict and catholicity. It is curious that with such an obvious theologian as the president of the conference, theology seems not to be on the horizon of the thinking reflected in the documents and reports.

There is also little apparent awareness of the rest of the church. Admittedly, this is a bishops' conference, and it is appropriate that the ministry of bishops should be in the foreground, but the picture of the church in the documents so far available seems innocent of the presence and role of clergy and laity. Yet catholicity is about the life of the church body as a whole, not just the service that bishops are called to give in the service of that body and its catholicity.

Nonetheless there was clearly direction of a general kind given in Williams' final presidential address. Like a conference facilitator, he reflected back to the conference the general perspective of the conference conversations in five succinct points. The address was widely and warmly approved by those present and reflects not just William's personal analytical capacity but also sensitivity to the sense of the conference. How far this re-invention of the Lambeth Conference will carry through to subsequent actions in worldwide Anglicanism is yet to be seen. While it did not open up significantly new horizons in dealing with the differences in the Anglican Communion, it certainly did not exacerbate those divisions, which could easily have happened, and it set out an approach to the problems in the Communion within a more fruitful perspective.

# 9

# Conflict, Catholicity, and Hope

FOR THE LAST THIRTY years, Anglican have been involved in a novel experiment of developing a workable Anglican ecclesiology in a supra-
provincial direction. Quite understandably, this has been a very difficult
experience, because Anglicans came to the late-twentieth century with
limited experience of working out an ecclesiology that reached beyond
the local province. For over a thousand years Anglicans and their predecessors had stoutly defended the local over against incursions from the
more imperial form of the Roman Catholic Church in Western Europe.
It is not surprising that when such a tradition faced within its own family the challenge of inter-provincial relations, it did not have readily to
hand a set of categories or a tradition of theological thought that could
be easily brought to bear. The current experiment has been conducted in
the usual way in the history of the church. Things have been tried and
attempts made to see how these steps might be understood in the light
of the theological tradition. Theological proposals have been made and
considered in the context of making sense of the life of the church and
how to be faithful to Christ in the moment.

This kind of development has become necessary for Anglicans because of the way in which they are now spread around the world in such
different locations and circumstances, and yet at the same time modern
communications has made them or at least some of them, instantly present to each other in words and images carried on the Internet. But they
come to this point in their history in the confluence of some very powerful
forces. These forces include the experience of being part of imperial powers past and present, of colonies past yet living on in present memories
and feelings, nationalism and underlying demographic changes in some
countries, and ethnic and tribal heritages in others. Wars and hostility

have affected the lived experience of many Anglicans. Also disturbing these waters have been globalization and its corporate imperialisms, the impact of atheistic materialism with its material goods and social uncertainties, conflicts of outlook in social life between modernity and traditional modes of thought, the resurgence of Islam in many parts of the world, and the extraordinary phenomenon of the major religions having to live cheek by jowl with each other. Not least of all by any means are the rapid growth of churches in the Global South and the decline of church attendance in the West. There are many forces at work and different trajectories taken across this field only go to show how dynamic these forces are. Anglicans are not alone among the Christian churches in facing these issues. Emigrations from home locations have in recent decades created the same kinds of challenges for Coptic and Orthodox Christians.

It should not be surprising therefore that Anglicans trying to work out how to relate to each other in this global environment should be having difficulties. Also not surprisingly, the present crisis over homosexuality in the public life of the church has raised a variety of other issues that were embedded in the different mentalities and cultures that the complex modern world had shaped. Apart from the challenge to live Christianly through this conflict, it is genuinely a crisis of imagination.

The present crisis elicited a response from the instruments of the Anglican Communion based on notions of communion and unity as set out in the Virginia Report and continued in the Windsor Report. The strategy was to manage the conflict by providing for some mechanism that would produce a degree of restraint and some agreed conformity of practice. The covenant proposed by Windsor was unacceptable, and a process of adjustment has not proved to be easy. That process is continuing and is offered by Rowan Williams not as an instrument of exclusion but as a means of identifying an intensification of belonging. The strategy inevitably involves some sense of levels of affiliation that in turn raises some difficult questions about relations between these levels and how movement between them can be achieved, especially if there is to be any retention of exclusive local ecclesiastical jurisdiction. This is a painful process as Anglicans try to sustain their own integrity and find ways of recognizing the integrity of others.

But it seems to me that the Anglican tradition of faith has not been very clear on the theme of the unity of the church, and its handling of that theme theologically and in practice has not been very good. The long history of intimate relations with the state has often confused Anglicans about the nature of Christian unity and made it easy for them to think of unity in terms of agreement or conformity. The sixteenth- and seventeenth-century reformations in England illustrate this very well. The religious renewal was established in legislative form by a government that was itself in the process of effecting a constitutional revolution that centralized the state upon the crown. The Church of England was caught up in this, and its formularies inherited from that time reflect that enmeshment. The struggle to undo this in the period between 1660 and 1662 only highlights the dramatic character of the revolution in theological understanding about the nature of the church effected by the 1662 Act of Uniformity.

In the longer run of Anglican sentiment, catholicity has been a more fruitful theme in ecclesiology. The long experience of local identity within a wider church fellowship prior to the eleventh century shaped the traditional mode of catholicity in Anglicanism and provided the basis of the English struggle with the increasingly imperial notions of church in the reforms of Pope Gregory VII. The triumph of national identity in Europe in the period after the fifteenth century put such a connected notion of catholicity out of reach, and people like Richard Hooker simply gave up on it as a practical possibility. Catholicity within a sub-tradition of Christianity like Anglicanism combines some very important elements for the present crisis of imagination for Anglicans. It asserts the presence of God in the church through the gifts that are given to the church for its life and mission. It locates the life of faith in the actual local context where Christians are called to be faithful. It highlights the fallibility of the church and of Christians in both practice and belief, in judgment and imagination. It sets the interdependence of the local and other locals of the wider church in the context of humility, and it sets the key issues of epistemology, authority, and discipleship in the context of eschatology, of hope.

Within Anglicanism, the language of catholicity has been used in many different senses. The same is true of the term unity. During the twentieth century, unity became a key term in ecumenical relations and as a consequence also in discussions about the nature of the church. The multivalent character of such terms as unity, catholicity, and communion points to a problem of communication and understanding. In different contexts these terms come with baggage that is not always clearly identified and yet is nonetheless potent in the meaning and weight attached to them. Clearing this up takes time and patience. There is also a methodological point involved as to how best to enter into a theological analysis of a problem.

How we approach any particular challenge is not always decisive, especially when we are concerned with complex and extensive issues. The present crisis involves many people around the world, and that brings to bear all sorts of possibilities, some of which in the light of history will turn out to be more helpful than others. That the present crisis has been approached through the window of unity and communion, and through the vehicle of a covenant, richly illustrates this. The initial covenant was clearly never going to work. The second, or Nassau, version was better but still lacked what is necessary to carry enough conviction from enough people. The St. Andrews version is better still, though it has some real problems. It is a long and I am sure tedious process, and some have tired of it. But it shows that having begun at a certain point it has proved necessary to move in directions that will engage with people who begin at a different place. Negotiating this and sustaining the conversation in the face of acted-out frustration is painful and difficult. That is the nature of such conversations, and they always call for patience and forbearance. My point here, however, is that wherever you start out on a theological issue you will have to take account of other elements in the tradition, since no starting point will adequately bear the complex richness of the divine presence in our ecclesial life to which we are responding.

With these kinds of qualifications I want to suggest some polarities that could frame a fruitful approach to this crisis. I set them out in some baldness in the first instance but wish to explain a little what I have in mind as a perspective for approaching our challenge.

| A | B |
|---|---|
| Catholicity | Unity |
| Conflict resolution | Conflict management |
| Network bridges | Institutional affiliation |
| Fallibility and modesty | Agreement and commitment |
| Personal faithfulness in context | General agreement for all contexts |
| Intermediate proximity | Global relations |

For reasons I shall try to explain, I think it is easier to get what we want in column B if we start from column A. Catholicity emphasizes the priority of the local and immediate setting of the call to be faithful, and that is sustained by engagement with other locals and the engaged whole. Both of these bring with them historical memory and institutions. It thus makes for a more dynamic and constructive movement between the whole, in this case worldwide Anglicanism, and the local. Rowan Williams made the point for catholicity in his final address at the 2008 Lambeth Conference. "The global horizon of the Church matters because churches without this are always in danger of slowly surrendering to the culture around them and losing sight of their calling to challenge that culture."[1] This is truly the key contemporary axis of the catholic principle, though it is not essentially a global concept but rather a concept that applies to the local church at whatever degree of extent. It is reflected in Paul's rebuke to the very local Corinthian church "For who sees anything different in you? What do you have that you did not receive? And if you received it, why do you boast as if were not a gift?" (1 Cor 4:7). It is expressed in the collection Paul initiated from the churches of the Aegean area for those in Jerusalem. In Anglican ecclesiology it has effectively been developed in institutional terms up to the extent of the province. That is how and why Anglicans have local provincial autonomy. But the extent of Anglicans around the world and the re-configuration of distance and proximity are the occasion for extending the terms of catholicity to the global for precisely the same reasons that apply within provinces and dioceses. Any given local is likely to become a caricature of itself, or as Williams says, risk "slowly surrendering to the culture around" them. They also risk becoming captive to the strengths in their own traditions to the point where those strengths become calcified.

Embracing the conflict and dealing with it directly would provide a better environment for winning agreement about general issues. It would also have the effect of not implying anything beyond the issues in the conflict that could and should be dealt with in their own terms. This would also better reflect the dynamics of Anglican catholicity. In any case it is something more that somewhat astonishing on any grounds that the current Anglican Communion instruments have not addressed the actual issue in conflict in the last ten years.

1. Williams, "Concluding Presidential Address."

Building network bridges and commencing with a sense of fallibility and modesty begins with the local and moves out and thus enables the nurturing of relationships which in turn enable catholicity to work effectively. Intermediate relations between the local and the global would provide for a more effective catholicity for Anglicans. Where proximity enhances the strength of relations and commonalities, distance without intermediate proximity diminishes both relationships and commonalities.

I am not suggesting that it is impossible to move in the other direction, the direction that in general terms has so far been adopted by the instruments of the Anglican Communion. Rather I am saying that starting from A and moving to B is more likely to be constructive, is more in keeping with a dynamic notion of catholicity that itself carries richer resources and less negative baggage in the Anglican tradition than notions of unity and communion.

These considerations relate to the path that might be taken in the present crisis. They do not themselves express a vision of how the Anglican Communion might be imagined. Rowan Williams considered this issue in his opening address at Lambeth and returned to it briefly in his final address, and I now turn to his analysis. In the opening address he began his discussion of imagined communions with a very clear statement of what he is most concerned about: "our greatest need in the Communion now is for transformed relationships." That concern is reflected in his hopes for the new the kind of Lambeth conference that he had just finished outlining. "Changed relationships" does not mean just warm feelings, but "new habits of respect, patience and understanding, and responsible agreement" and "search for the common mind, in constant active involvement in the life of other parts of the family." For bishops especially it means "shared commitments to a rule of life and a pattern of prayer so that it remains possible to see in the other person another believer, another redeemed sinner, another person on the way to transformation in Christ."[2] From the point of view of trying to engage with the current crisis in the Communion, it would be hard to think of a more appropriate starting point.

In that theme he then recognizes the hurt and perplexity manifest in the present conflicts. He notes the pressures created by new structures that have been improvised, by which he seems to mean the cross-border

2. Williams, "Archbishop's First Presidential Address."

consecrations and the creation of networks across provincial boundaries on matters to do with ordained ministry that have traditionally been the responsibility of each province. There may also be a hint here of the changes envisaged by GAFCON. Of course, these have not been the only structural innovations. The development of the Primates meeting and some of its purported actions are also innovations that are quite disturbing for many in the Communion. The focus on the so called Instruments of Unity in the Communion as having some kind of de facto institutional monopoly or presumed pre-eminence is also a considerable innovation. Even the enhanced position of the office of the Archbishop of Canterbury as some kind of *primus inter pares* amongst primates is new, as is the idea that communion with the Archbishop of Canterbury defines what it is to be Anglican. As a matter of historical fact, the first Lambeth Conference was called for bishops whose churches were in communion with the Church of England, and quite a number of existing provinces in the Anglican Communion define their connection not in terms of the Archbishop of Canterbury, but with the Church of England, which is not quite the same thing. Rowan Williams is quite right in his basic assertion, even if the apparent scope of his remark should be widened somewhat. There have been innovations, and not surprisingly they have caused perplexity and often deep concern and hurt, and in some cases they are hard to defend out of Anglican history.

Williams then offers three possible models of the Communion that are attractive to different theological dispositions but which he finds lacking.

1. A loose federation, perhaps with diverse expression of Anglicanism existing side by side in more or less open competition but with little co-ordination of mission, little sense of obligation to sustain a common set of theological and practical commitments.

Such open competition he says would hardly be a federation and would encourage unappealing religious division.

2. Simply a family of regional or national churches strictly demarcated from each other—sovereign states, as it were, with independent systems of government, coming together from time to time for matters of common concern.

This he points out ignores the complexities of a globalized society and economy and does not make sense of the biblical and historical sense of churches learning from each other.

3. A firmer and more consistent control of diversity, a more effective set of bodies to govern the local communities making up the Communion.

This he claims could be at the mercy of powerfully motivated groups who wanted to redefine the basic terms of belonging so that Anglicanism became confessional in a way that he thinks it has never been.

All of these models embody something from the history of Anglicanism. There have been a few examples of the kind of competition within particular areas referred to in the first model. Anglican mission agencies competed for locations in the past, and there is competing and overlapping Anglicanism in Europe between churches from the Church of England and The Episcopal Church. For historic reasons there is some overlap in the Philippines. The non-Jurors of the seventeenth century in England persisted as a separate Anglican group in England. But all these are clearly oddities, and the notion of such competition is certainly outside the ordinary sense of Anglican polity. The second model reflects the sense of isolation that was part of the reasons for calling the first Lambeth Conference and which in part motivated the Anglican Congresses. The third reflects the aberration of the Royal Supremacy in sixteenth-century England and the kind of imagined Roman Catholicism that Anglicans have spent a millennium rejecting.

So clearly Williams is right in his criticisms. Nonetheless each example includes something that could be part of an imagined Anglican Communion. There could be some greater degree of collaboration and entry into otherwise highly protected jurisdictional territories. Any notion of interdependence would seem to suggest that. Exchange and partnership arrangements already exist by mutual agreement. Some sense of provincial autonomy is surely part of the Anglican heritage and embodies something about the commitment to the local within a context of wider interdependence. Reciprocal catholicity does not work without some sense of differentiation. The impact of the globalized world undoubtedly has an effect upon the notion of the local and any Anglican catholicity will need to come to terms with this changed situation. Rowan Williams is quite correct to draw attention to this new reality.

This leaves the fourth option that Williams commends. His key words are "council and covenant." He sets this vision out in an elegant and attractive paragraph.

> It is the vision of an Anglicanism whose diversity is limited not by centralised control but by consent—consent based on a serious *common* assessment of the implications of local change. How do we genuinely think *together* about diverse local challenges? If we can find ways of answering this, we shall have discovered an Anglicanism in which prayerful consultation is routine and accepted and understood as part of what is entailed in belonging to a fellowship that is more than local. The entire Church is present in every local church assembled around the Lord's Table. Yet the local church alone is never the entire Church. We are called to see this not as a circle to be squared but as an invitation to be more and more lovingly engaged with each other.

This is in my view a genuine and attractive statement of the kind of catholicity that is embedded in the long tradition of Anglican faith. But the problem is how do Anglicans get there and what would such a vision look life in institutional terms. Also how would it embody some other elements in Anglican ecclesial thought and practice? How would it embody a tradition of conciliarism? Is the current set of global instruments adequately ecclesial in character, or do they suffer from being too narrowly episcopal? How would conflict be dealt with when extended conversation had unearthed it or when actions by one or another province displayed it?

Rowan Williams strongly supports the covenant as a way to advance towards this vision. Clearly there has been some serious development of the covenant, but it has a long way to go before it will bring large numbers, or even all those provinces who might want to affirm a particular view about homosexuality one way or the other. The problem with the covenant process, especially in the light of its history so far, is that it draws to the surface other issues besides the place of homosexuality in the public life of the church. Those issues can hide behind the homosexuality issue and can encourage, indeed appear already to have encouraged, significant institutional reactions. So while I can embrace Williams' vision on the grounds of catholicity, I have some difficulty with the covenant strategy. That does not mean that the process should not continue. It might eventually lead to something good, since those involved in the design process have been highly consultative and open.

The vision of catholicity set out here, and as it seems to be emerging from the covenant process, looks like leading to a tiered form of connection or affiliation. Depending on whether GAFCON develops into a competing ecclesiastical system, you would then finish up with a set of Covenant groups in tiered affiliation, which would presumably grow as different issues of conflict and decision arose so that on one issue you might be in one level of acceptance and on another issue in a different level. The covenant group would presumably claim to be the Anglican communion, or to represent "true" or "historic" Anglicanism. GAFCON would presumably make similar claims as to its identity. So Anglicanism would become a contested claim in relation to what had become clear institutional entities. This would I hope be the worst-case scenario and I would much prefer the covenant process to produce something more genuinely encompassing.

But having said that, it seems to me there is another vision of a possible Anglican Communion that could express what I will call the gospel catholicity that Rowan Williams has so elegantly expressed and to which I have referred earlier. This vision would involve reducing the demand for institutional affiliation. It would move the situation back a little historically and seek for global models of connection that were more in the nature of facilitating networks. It would be more conciliar in nature and find ways of embracing the whole people of God in the cultivation of interdependent and respectful catholicity in the church. In that respect it might go back to instruments like the congresses or shared arrangements for theological educational and research. It would act in relation to conflicts that arose in their particular situations and with the groups and provinces engaged. It would be more inclined to confront conflict and to deal with it in a way that focused on the actual issue and engaged it with the lived Christian realities of those involved and the tradition of faith and practice that constitutes the historical definition of Anglicanism.

There is a well-known story about the traveler who had lost his way and asked a local how to get to such-and-such a town. The local replied that if he wanted to get there he would not be starting here. Part of me feels that if we wanted to get to such a vision of the Anglican Communion we would not start where we are. But that is clearly not realistic, even if it does suggest the need for some demystification of recent institutional innovations. But it does seem to me that there are some things that could begin to bring forward such a model. We could actually engage immediately with the current conflict over homosexuality. There are good theologians on both sides of this argument. Why could they not be brought together? Some Global South provinces have declared they are not in communion with The Episcopal Church in the USA and the Anglican Church of Canada. Why not bring them together and facilitate a real theological and ecclesial engagement? Why not try facilitating engagement rather than arbitration? The ACC identifies networks of various kinds and recognizes that they are part of the institutions of the Anglican Communion. Why not extend the range of such recognitions? Incorporate networks that foster connections and engagement across local differences. Make manifest the rich diversity of connections that hold Anglicans together around the world under the umbrella of the one institution that has a conciliar character and a constitution agreed by the provinces and can claim to be representative of those Anglican provinces.

Regional groups of provinces already exist. Such groupings could provide the intermediate connections that would grow catholic interdependence between provinces through more effective mutual engagement. Asia, North America, Europe, and the Middle East, the whole of Africa, Central and South America could provide five regions to start thinking about. It could build on existing arrangements, though some changes would be necessary. Whether these turn out to be the best groupings to facilitate and grow appropriate catholicity is not as important as the project of growing interdependence in life and mission from the local out.

In one sense this would be institutionally a lower profile and a looser-limbed version of catholicity, but it might turn out to be less divisive and more cohering than tighter institutional affiliations. It might in that sense sustain catholicity and some more open and worthwhile sense of Anglican identity. It would probably be harder work and it would give a quite distinctive orientation to the work of a bishop as an instrument of unity in the church. It would also be culturally challenging in the current global environment which increasingly tends to the organizationally coercive. It certainly would not be a case of Anglicans "slowly surrendering to the culture around them and losing sight of their calling to challenge that culture." it would provide some prospect of engaging with both the fallible realities of our personal and ecclesial life and with the redeeming action and continuing presence of the crucified Christ and the hope of the kingdom of God. It would also be more consistent with the heritage of Anglican faith and practice of which the current generation is both the heir and the steward.

# Bibliography

THIS BIBLIOGRAPHY GIVES THE full details of references in the footnotes of the text.

The text of the Lambeth Conferences can be found along with a great deal of other useful documentation on the Anglican Communion portal at http://www.anglicancommunion.org/

Alexander, C. F. *Hymns for Little Children*. London: H. Rowsell, 1859.

Anglican Communion. "Primates' Meeting February 2005 Communiqué." Report on the Anglican Communion Primates' Meeting held at the Dromantine Retreat and Conference Centre, Newry, in Northern Ireland, February 20–25, 2005. Online: http://www.anglicancommunion.org/communion/primates/resources/downloads/communique%20_english.pdf

Anglican Communion Committee. "The Anglican Communion." The Lambeth Conference 1948: The Encyclical Letter from the Bishops; together with Resolutions and Reports, 81–98. London: SPCK, 1948.

Anglican Consultative Council. "A Final Report from the International Anglican Conversations on Human Sexuality." Online: http://www.aco.org/listening/resources/conversations_on_human_sexuality.pdf.

———. "'Towards an Anglican Covenant': A Consultation Paper on the Covenant Proposal of the Windsor Report." Online: http://www.anglicancommunion.org/commission/covenant/consultation/index.cfm.

Anglican Communion News Service. "Archbishop sets out thinking on Lambeth Conference 2008." March 9, 2006. Online: http://www.anglicancommunion.org/acns/news.cfm/2006/3/9/ACNS4127.

———. "First invitations to 'reflective and learning-based' Lambeth Conference go out." May 22, 2007. Online: http://www.anglicancommunion.org/acns/news.cfm/2007/5/22/ACNS4287.

Anglican Consultative Council and Inter-Anglican Theological and Doctrinal Commission. *For the Sake of the Kingdom: God's Church and the New Creation*. London: Published for the Anglican Consultative Council by Church House, 1986.

Atkinson, A. *The Europeans in Australia: A History. Volume One, The Beginning*. Melbourne: Oxford University Press, 1997.

———. *The Europeans in Australia: A History. Volume Two, Democracy*. Melbourne: Oxford University Press, 2004.

Austin, A. *Australian Education, 1788–1900: Church, State and Public Education in Colonial Australia*. Melbourne: Pitman, 1961.

# Bibliography

Avis, P. D. L. *Beyond the Reformation?: Authority, Primacy and Unity in the Conciliar Tradition*. London: T. & T. Clark, 2006.

Bardesanes, and H. J. W. Drijvers. *The Book of the Laws of Countries: Dialogue on the Fate of Bardaisan of Edessa*. Assen: Van Gorcum, 1965.

Barth, K. *Church Dogmatics*. Vol. 1, *The Doctrine of the Word of God, Part 1*. Edinburgh: T. & T. Clark, 1975.

————. *Protestant Theology in the Nineteenth Century: Its Background & History*. London: SCM, 1972.

Battle, M. *Reconciliation: The Ubuntu Theology of Desmond Tutu*. Cleveland, OH: Pilgrim, 1997.

Bauckham, R., editor. *The Gospels for All Christians: Rethinking the Gospel Audiences*. Grand Rapids: Eerdmans, 1998.

Bianchi, E., and R. Ruether, editors. *A Democratic Church: The Reconstruction of Roman Catholicism*. New York: Crossroad, 1992.

Broughton, W. G. *Diary Kept During the Voyage of the Ship John from England to New South Wales*. In Correspondence and diary of William Grant Broughton. Sydney: State Library of New South Wales, 1829.

————. *Speech of the Lord Bishop of Australia in the Legislative Council upon the Resolution for Establishing a System of General Education*. Sydney: Tegg, 1839.

Bridge, C. "Review Essay: Bishop Broughton's Education Policy and the Historians." *Australian and New Zealand History of Education Society Journal* 9 (1981) 55–62.

Brooke, C. N. L. "Gregorian Reforms in Action: Clerical Marriage in England, 1050–1200." *Cambridge Historical Journal* 12 (1956) 1–21.

Brown, P. *The Rise of Western Christendom: Triumph and Diversity AD 200–1000*. Oxford: Blackwell, 1996.

Cable, K. "Religious Controversies in New South Wales in the Mid-Nineteenth Century. Aspects of Anglicanism, 1848–1850." *Journal of the Royal Australian Historical Society* 49 (1963) 58–74.

————. "The University of Sydney and Its Affiliated College, 1850–1880." *The Australian University* 2 (1964) 183–214.

Campbell, W. S. *Paul's Gospel in an Intercultural Context: Jew and Gentile in the Letter to the Romans*. New York: Lang, 1991.

Carter, S. *The Culture of Disbelief: How American Law and Politics Trivialize Religious Devotion*. New York: Anchor Doubleday, 1993.

————. *The Dissent of the Governed: A Meditation on Law, Religion and Loyalty*. Cambridge: Harvard University Press, 1998.

————. *God's Name in Vain: The Wrongs and Rights of Religion in Politics*. New York: Basic, 2000.

Catholic Church. Synod Extraordinary (1985: Rome Italy). *A Message to the People of God; and, the Final Report*. Washington DC: National Conference of Catholic Bishops, 1986.

Chapman, M. "Where Is It All Going? A Plea for Humility." In *A Fallible Church: Lambeth Essays*, edited by K. Stevenson, 122–41. London: Darton Longman & Todd, 2008.

Charlesworth, H. *Writing in Rights: Australia and the Protection of Human Rights*. Sydney: University of New South Wales Press, 2002.

Church of Nigeria (Anglican Commmunion). "Message to the Nation/Communiqué." February 2006. Online: http://www.anglican-nig.org/communique_ibadan2006.htm.

Claydon, T., and I. McBride. "The Trials of the Chosen Peoples: Recent Interpretations of Protestantism and National Identity in Britain and Ireland." In *Protestantism and National Identity: Britain and Ireland, C.1650–1850*, edited by T. Claydon and I. McBride, 3–32. Cambridge: Cambridge University Press, 1998.

"The Church, in the Word of God, Celebrates the Mysteries of Christ for the Salvation of the World." Second Extraordinary Synod. Final Report of the 1985 Synod, Rome, 1985. Online: http://www.saint-mike.org/Library/Synod_Bishops/Final_Report1985.html.

Cnattingius, H. *Bishops and Societies. A Study of Anglican Colonial and Missionary Expansion 1689-1850*. London: SPCK, 1952.

Congar, Y. *The Meaning of Tradition*. New York: Hawthorn, 1964.

Congar, Y., and A. V. Littledale. *The Mystery of the Church*. Baltimore: Helicon, 1960.

Covenant Design Group of the Anglican Communion. "An Anglican Covenant Draft." April 2007. Online: http://www.anglicancommunion.org/commission/covenant/report/draft_text.cfm.

Cowdrey, H. E. J. *Lanfranc: Scholar, Monk, and Archbishop*. Oxford: Oxford University Press, 2003.

———. *Popes and Church Reform in the 11th Century*. Aldershot, UK: Ashgate, 2000.

Cross, C. *Church and People, 1450–1660: The Triumph of the Laity in the English Church*. London: Collins Fontana, 1976.

Cumbrae-Stewart, F. "Section 116 of the Constitution." *Australian Law Journal* 20 (1946) 207–12.

Curtis, M. "The Hampton Court Conference and Its Aftermarth." *History* 46 (1961).

Davies, W. *The Gospel and the Land: Early Christianity and Jewish Territorial Doctrine*. Berkeley: University of California Press, 1974.

Davison, G., S. Macintyre, J. B. Hirst, H. Doyle, and K. Torney. *The Oxford Companion to Australian History*. Melbourne: Oxford University Press, 1998.

Daw, E. D. "Church and State in the Empire: The Conference of Australian Bishops, 1850." *Journal of Imperial and Commonwealth History* 5 (1977) 251–69.

———. *Church and State in the Empire: The Evolution of Imperial Policy, 1846–1856*. Canberra: Department of Government, Faculty of Military Studies, University of New South Wales Press, 1977.

Dearmer, P., and A. Jacob. *Songs of Praise Discussed: A Handbook to the Best-Known Hymns and to Others Recently Introduced*. London: Oxford University Press, 1933.

Donaldson, T. L. *Paul and the Gentiles: Remapping the Apostle's Convictional World*. Minneapolis: Fortress, 1997.

Donfried, K. P. *The Romans Debate*. Edinburgh: T. & T. Clark, 1991.

Douglas, D. C., and G. W. Greenaway, editors. *English Historical Documents*. London: Eyre and Spottiswood, 1953–1956.

Douglas, I. T. "Authority after Colonialism." *The Witness* 83 (2000) 10–14.

Douglas, I. T., and K. Pui-lan. *Beyond Colonial Anglicanism: The Anglican Communion in the Twenty-first Century*. New York: Church, 2001.

Dunn, J. D. G. *Romans*. Work Biblical Commentary 38. Dallas: Word, 1988.

Ehrman, B. D. *The Apostolic Fathers*. 2 vols. Cambridge: Harvard University Press, 2003.

Ely, R. *Unto God and Caesar: Religious Issues in the Emerging Commonwealth, 1891–1906*. Melbourne: Melbourne University Press, 1976.

Evans, B. N. *Interpreting the Free Exercise of Religion: The Constitution and American Pluralism*. Chapel Hill: University of North Carolina Press, 1997.

# Bibliography

Fletcher, E. F. *Benedict Biscop*. Durham: Jarrow Lecture 24, 1981.

Fortescue, S. J. *On the Laws and Governance of England*. Cambridge: Cambridge University Press, 1997.

Frame, T. R. *Anglicans in Australia*. Sydney: University of New South Wales Press, 2007.

———. *Church and State: Australia's Imaginary Wall*. Sydney: University of New South Wales Press, 2006.

Gardner, J. F. *Family and Familia in Roman Law and Life*. Oxford: Clarendon, 1998.

Gascoigne, J. "Church and State Unified: Hooker's Rationale for the English Post-Reformation Order." *Journal of Religious History* 21 (1997) 23–34.

———. "The Unity of Church and State Challenged: Responses to Hooker from the Restoration to the Nineteenth-Century Age of Reform." *Journal of Religious History* 21 (1997) 60–79.

Georgi, D. *Remembering the Poor: The History of Paul's Collection for Jerusalem*. Nashville: Abingdon, 1992.

Giles, K. *The Trinity and Subordinationism: The Doctrine of God and the Contemporary Gender Debate*. Downers Grove, IL: InterVarsity, 2002.

Green, J. B., and M. C. Mckeever. *Luke-Acts and New Testament Historiography*. Grand Rapids: Baker, 1994.

Greenman, J. P., and T. Larsen. *Reading Romans Through the Centuries: From the Early Church to Karl Barth*. Grand Rapids: Brazos, 2005.

Grieb, A. K. "Interpreting the Proposed Anglican Covenant through the Communiqué." Delivered before the House of Bishops on March 19, 2007. Online: http://www.episcopalchurch.org/78650_84227_ENG_HTM.htm.

———. *The Story of Romans: A Narrative Defense of God's Righteousness*. Louisville: Westminster John Knox, 2002.

Grislis, E. "The Role of Consensus in Richard Hooker's Theological Enquiry." In *The Heritage of Christian Thought: Essays in Honor of Robert Lowry Calhoun*, edited by E. Cushman Re and Grislis, 64–88. New York: Harper & Row, 1965.

Harris, W. *An Historical and Critical Account of the Life of Charles the Second, King of Great Britain, after the Manner of Mr Bayle, . . . To Which Is Added an Appendix of Original Papers, Etc, 2 Vols*. London: Millar, 1766.

Hartz, L. *The Founding of New Societies*. San Diego: Harcourt Brace Jovanovich, 1964.

Hauerwas, S. *After Christendom?: How the Church Is to Behave If Freedom, Justice, and a Christian Nation Are Bad Ideas*. Nashville: Abingdon, 1991.

———. *A Community of Character: Toward a Constructive Christian Social Ethic*. Notre Dame, IN: University of Notre Dame Press, 1981.

Hauerwas, S., J. Berkman, and M. G. Cartwright. *The Hauerwas Reader*. Durham, NC: Duke University Press, 2001.

Hegarty, A., and S. Leonard. *Human Rights: An Agenda for the 21st Century*. London: Cavendish, 1999.

Hill, C., and E. Yarnold, S.J., editors. *Anglicans and Roman Catholics: The Search for Unity*. London: SPCK/CTS, 1994.

Hill, E. *Ministry and Authority in the Catholic Church*. London: Cassell, 1988.

Holmes, D. L. *The Faiths of the Founding Fathers*. New York: Oxford University Press, 2006.

Hooker, Richard. *The Folger Library Edition of the Works of Richard Hooker*. Edited by W. Speed Hill. 7 vols. Cambridge and Binghampton: Harvard University Press and Medieval and Renaissance Studies, 1977–1998.

Hutton, R. *The Restoration: A Political and Religious History of England and Wales, 1658–1667*. Oxford: Clarendon, 1985.

Inglis, K. S. *Australian Colonists: An Exploration of Social History, 1788–1870*. Carlton, Victoria: Melbourne University Press, 1993.

Inter-Anglican Theological and Doctrinal Commission. *Communion, Conflict and Hope*. London: The Anglican Communion Office, 2008. Online: http://www .anglicancommunion.org/ministry/theological/iatdc/docs/communion_ conflict_&_hope.pdf.

———. "Responding to a proposal of a covenant—October 2006." Online: http://www .aco.org/ministry/theological/iatdc/docs/2006covenant.cfm.

Isaac, R. "'The Rage of Malice of the Old Serpent Devil': The Dissenters and the Making and Remaking of the Virginia Statute for Religious Freedom." In *The Virginia Statute for Religious Freedom: Its Evolution and Consequences in American History*, edited by M. D. Peterson, R. C. Vaughan, and Virginia Foundation for the Humanities and Public Policy, 139–69. Cambridge: Cambridge University Press, 1988.

———. *The Transformation of Virginia, 1740–1790*. Chapel Hill: Published for the Institute of Early American History and Culture, Williamsburg, VA, University of North Carolina Press, 1982.

Jacob, W. *The Making of the Anglican Church Worldwide*. London: SPCK, 1997.

Jefferson, T., and M. D. Peterson. *Writings*. New York: Literary Classics of the U.S., 1984.

Jefferson, Thomas, and Merrill D. Peterson. *Writings*, Library of America;. New York: Literary Classics of the U.S., 1984.

Jenkins, Philip. *The Next Christendom: The Rise of Global Christianity*. Oxford; New York: Oxford University Press, 2002.

Jewett, Robert. *Romans: A Commentary*. Assisted by Roy D. Kotansky. Edited by Eldon Jay Epp. Hermeneia—A Critical and Historical Commentary on the Bible. Minneapolis: Fortress, 2007.

Jordan, W. K. *The Development of Religious Toleration in England*. London: Allen & Unwin, 1936.

Kaye, B. N. *The Argument of Romans with Special Reference to Chapter 6*. Austin: Schola, 1979.

———. "An Australian Definition of Religion." *University of New South Wales Law Journal* 14 (1992) 332–51.

———. *An Introduction to World Anglicanism*. Cambridge: Cambridge University Press, 2008.

———. "Power, Order and Plurality: Getting Together in the Anglican Communion." *Journal of Anglican Studies* 2 (2004) 81–95.

———. *Reinventing Anglicanism: A Vision of Confidence, Community and Engagement in Anglican Christianity*. Adelaide: Openbook, 2004.

———. "The Strange Birth of Anglican Synods in Australia and the 1850 Bishop's Conference." *Journal of Religious History* 27 (2003) 177–97.

———. "'To the Romans and Others' Revisited." *Novum Testamentum* 18 (1976) 37–77.

———. "Unity in the Anglican Communion: A Critique of the 'Virginia Report.'" *St Mark's Review* 184 (2001) 24–32.

———. *Web of Meaning: The Role of Origins in Christian Faith*. Sydney: Aquila, 2000.

Kaye, B. N., editor. *Anglicanism in Australia: A History*. Melbourne: Melbourne University Press, 2002.

# Bibliography

Kingdom, J. *No Such Thing as Society? Individualism and Community*. Buckingham: Open University Press, 1992.

Kinnamon, M. E., editor. *Signs of the Spirit: Official Report Seventh Assembly, Canberra, Australia*. Geneva: WCC, 1991.

Kociumbas, J. *The Oxford History of Australia*. Vol. 2, *1770–1860: Possessions*. Melbourne: Oxford University Press, 1995.

Kung, H. *My Struggle for Freedom: Memoirs*. Grand Rapids: Eerdmans, 2003.

Lambeth Conference (1988). *The Truth Shall Make You Free: The Lambeth Conference 1988: The Reports, Resolutions & Pastoral Letters from the Bishops*. London: Published for the Anglican Consultative Council by Church House Publishing, 1988.

Lane Fox, R. *Pagans and Christians*. London: Allen & Unwin, 1987.

Lane, P. *The Australian Federal System, with United States Analogues*. Sydney: 1972.

Limerick, D., B. Cunnington, and F. Crowther. *Managing the New Organisation: Collaboration and Sustainability in the Postcorporate World*. Sydney: Business and Professional Publishing, 1998.

Little, D. "Religion and Civil Virtue in America: Jefferson's Statute Reconsidered." In *The Virginia Statute for Religious Freedom: Its Evolution and Consequences in American History*, edited by M. D. Peterson, R. C. Vaughan, and Virginia Foundation for the Humanities and Public Policy, 139–69. Cambridge: Cambridge University Press, 1988.

Lubac, Henri de. *The Splendour of the Church*. New York: Sheed & Ward, 1956.

Luhmann, N. *Social Systems*. Stanford: Stanford University Press, 1995.

Lumb, R. *The Constitutions of the Australian States*. St. Lucia: University of Queensland Press, 1991.

Luscombe, D. "The 'Lex Divinitatis' in the Bull 'Unam Sanctam' of Pope Boniface Viii." In *Church and Government in the Middle Ages: Essays Presented to C. R. Cheney on His 70th Birthday*, edited by C. N. L. B. E. Al., 205–21. Cambridge: Cambridge University Press, 1976.

MacIntyre, A. *After Virtue: A Study in Moral Theory*. London: Duckworth, 1981.

MacMullen, R. *Paganism in the Roman Empire*. New Haven: Yale University Press, 1981.

Maddox, M. *God under Howard. The Rise of the Religious Right in Australian Politics*. Sydney: Allen and Unwin, 2005.

Markey, J. L. *Creating Communion. The Theology of the Constitutions of the Church*. New York: New City, 2003.

Martin, R. P. *Carmen Christi: Philippians Ii 5-11 in Recent Interpretation and in the Setting of Early Christian Worship*. Grand Rapids: Eerdmans, 1983.

Marty, M. E. "The Virginia Statute Two Hundred Years Later." In *The Virginia Statute for Religious Freedom: Its Evolution and Consequences in American History*, edited by M. D. Peterson, R. C. Vaughan, and Virginia Foundation for the Humanities and Public Policy, 1–21. Cambridge: Cambridge University Press, 1988.

McDonald, L. M., and J. A. Sanders. *The Canon Debate*. Peabody, MA: Hendrickson, 2002.

McGrade, A. "The Coherence of Hooker's Polity: The Books on Power." *Journal of the History of Ideas* 24 (1963) 163–82.

———. "Introduction to Book VIII." In *The Folger Library Edition of the Works of Richard Hooker*, edited by W. E. Speed Hill, 337–94. Cambridge: Harvard University Press and Medieval and Renaissance Studies, 1993.

Metzger, Bruce M., and Bart D. Ehrman. *The Text of the New Testament: Its Transmission, Corruption, and Restoration*. 4th ed. New York: Oxford University Press, 2005.

Milton, J. *A Treatise of Civil Power in Ecclesiastical Causes Microform: Shewing That It Is Not Lawfull for Any Power on Earth to Compell in Matters of Religion.* London: Newcomb, 1659.

Milton, J., and J. A. St. John. *Select Prose Works of Milton.* London: Hatchard, 1836.

Moo, D. J. *Encountering the Book of Romans: A Theological Survey.* Grand Rapids: Baker Academic, 2002.

Morrill, J. S. *Revolution and Restoration: England in the 1650s.* London: Collins & Brown, 1992.

Moule, C. "Further Reflexions on Philippians 2:1–11." In *Apostolic History and the Gospel: Biblical and Historical Essays Presented to F. F. Bruce on His 60th Birthday,* edited by W. Gasque and R. Martin, 264–76. Exeter: Paternoster, 1970.

Ndungane, N. "Scripture: What is at Issue in Anglicanism Today?" *Anglican Theological Review* 83 (2001) 11–23.

Office of Communication, the Episcopal Church Center. *To Set Our Hope on Christ: A Response to the Invitation of Windsor Report Para 135.* New York: The Episcopal Church, 2005.

Olmstead, W. G. *Matthew's Trilogy of Parables: The Nation, the Nations and the Reader in Matthew 21:28—22:14.* Cambridge: Cambridge University Press, 2003.

Ottosson, D. "State-Sponsored Homophobia: A World Survey of Laws Prohibiting Same Sex Activity between Consenting Adults May 2008." International Lesbian and Gay Association, 2008. Available online at: www.ilga.org.

Parratt, J. *A Reader in African Christian Theology.* London: SPCK, 1997.

———. *Reinventing Christianity: African Theology Today.* Grand Rapids: Eerdmans, 1995.

Parsons, J. *The Church in the Republic: Gallicanism & Political Ideology in Renaissance France.* Washington DC: Catholic University of America Press, 2004.

Pelikan, J. *The Vindication of Tradition.* New Haven: Yale University Press, 1984.

Peterson, M. D., R. C. Vaughan, and Virginia Foundation for the Humanities and Public Policy. *The Virginia Statute for Religious Freedom: Its Evolution and Consequences in American History.* Cambridge: Cambridge University Press, 1988.

Pfeffer, L. "Maddison's "Detached Memoranda": Then and Now." In *The Virginia Statute for Religious Freedom: Its Evolution and Consequences in American History,* edited by M. D. Peterson, R. C. Vaughan and Virginia Foundation for the Humanities and Public Policy, 139–69. Cambridge: Cambridge University Press, 1988.

Pocock, J. G. A. "Religious Freedom and the Desacralization of Politics: From the English Civil Wars to the Virginia Statute." In *The Virginia Statute for Religious Freedom: Its Evolution and Consequences in American History,* edited by M. D. Peterson, R. C. Vaughan, and Virginia Foundation for the Humanities and Public Policy, 43–74. Cambridge: Cambridge University Press, 1988.

Poguntke, T., and P. Webb, editor. *The Presidentialization of Politics: A Comparative Study of Modern Democracies.* Oxford: Oxford University Press, 2004.

Pritchard, R. *A History of the Episcopal Church.* Harrisburg, PA: Morehouse, 1991.

Radner, E., and A. Goddard. "Human Rights, Homosexuality and the Anglican Communion: Reflections in Light of Nigeria." London: Fulcrum website, 2006. Online: http://www.fulcrum-anglican.org.uk/?167.

Rahner, K., editor. *Encyclopedia of Theology. The Concise Sacramentum Mundi.* Tunbridge Wells: Burns & Oates, 1993.

# Bibliography

Rivers, I. *Reason, Grace, and Sentiment: A Study of the Language of Religion and Ethics in England, 1660-1780*. Cambridge: Cambridge University Press, 1991.

Roberts, A., and J. Donaldson. *The Ante-Nicene Fathers; Translations of the Writings of the Fathers down to A.D. 325*. Grand Rapids: Eerdmans, 1950.

Rorty, R. "The Priority of Democracy to Philosophy." In *The Virginia Statute for Religious Freedom: Its Evolution and Consequences in American History*, edited by M. D. Peterson, R. C. Vaughan, and Virginia Foundation for the Humanities and Public Policy, 257–83. Cambridge: Cambridge University Press, 1988.

Rousseau, J.-J. *The Social Contract*. Harmondsworth, UK: Penguin, 1968.

Sanneh, L. O. *Encountering the West: Christianity and the Global Cultural Process: the African Dimension*. Maryknoll, NY: Orbis, 1993.

———. *Whose Religion is Christianity? The Gospel Beyond the West*. Grand Rapids: Eerdmans, 2003.

Schweitzer, A., and W. Montgomery. *The Mysticism of Paul the Apostle*. New York: Macmillan, 1956.

Shaw, G. "Judeo-Christianity and the Mid-Nineteenth Century Colonial Civil Order." In *Re-Visioning Australian Colonial Christianity: New Essays in the Australian Christian Experience 1788-1900*, edited by M. Hutchison and E. Campion, 29–39. Sydney: Centre for the Study of Australian Christianity, 1994.

———. *Patriarch and Patriot: William Grant Broughton, 1788–1853*. Melbourne: Melbourne University Press, 1978.

Shils, E. *Tradition*. London: Faber & Faber, 1981.

Skinner, Q. "What Does It Mean to Be a Free Person?" *London Review of Books* 30.10 (2008) 16–18.

Spurr, J. *The Restoration Church of England, 1646–1689*. New Haven: Yale University Press, 1991.

Stark, R. *The Rise of Christianity: A Sociologist Reconsiders History*. San Francisco: HarperCollins, 1997.

Stark, R., and R. Finke. *Acts of Faith: Explaining the Human Side of Religion*. Berkeley: University of California Press, 2000.

Stenschke, C. W. *Luke's Portrait of Gentiles Prior to Their Coming to Faith*. Tubingen: Mohr/Siebeck, 1999.

Stephenson, A. M. G. *Anglicanism and the Lambeth Conferences*. Foreword by the Archbishop of Canterbury. London: SPCK, 1976.

———. *The First Lambeth Conference, 1867*. Published for the Church Historical Society. London: SPCK, 1967.

Sterling, G. E. *Historiography and Self-Definition: Josephus, Luke-Acts and Apologetic Historiography*. Novum Testamentum Supplements 64. Leiden: Brill, 1992.

Stevenson, K. *A Fallible Church: Lambeth Essays*. London: Darton Longman & Todd, 2008.

Stump, P. *The Reforms of the Council of Constance (1414–1418)*. Leiden: Brill, 1994.

Tanner, N., editor. *Decrees of the Ecumenical Councils*. Washington: Georgetown University Press, 1990.

Taylor, S., C. Haydon, and J. Walsh. *The Church of England, C. 1689—C. 1833: From Toleration to Tractarianism*. Cambridge: Cambridge University Press, 1993.

Thomas, P. H. E. "Unity and Concord: An Early Anglican 'Communion' " *Journal of Anglican Studies* 2 (2004) 9–21.

Trigg, S. *Medievalism and the Gothic in Australian Culture*. Carlton, Victoria: Melbourne University Publishing, 2006.

Turney, C., U. Bygott, and P. Chippendale. *Australia's First: A History of the University of Sydney Volume I 1850–1939*. Sydney: Hale & Iremonger, 1991.

Tutu, D. *No Future without Forgiveness*. New York: Doubleday, 1999.

Veliz, C. *The New World of the Gothic Fox: Culture and Economy in English and Spanish America*. Berkeley: University of California Press, 1994.

Volf, M. *After Our Likeness: The Church as the Image of the Trinity*. Grand Rapids: Eerdmans, 1998.

Ward, J. M. *The State and the People: Australian Federation and Nation-Making, 1870-1901*. Sydney: Federation, 2001.

Watson, F., and P. Chapman, editor. *Historical Records of Australia*. 33 vols. Sydney: Library Committee of the Commonwealth Parliament, 1914–25, 1997.

Wilson, S. G. *The Gentiles and the Gentile Mission in Luke-Acts*. Society for New Testament Studies Monograph Series 23. Cambridge: Cambridge University Press, 1973.

Williams, Rowan. "The Archbishop Opens the Lambeth Conference." Lambeth Conference of the Anglican Communion, London, England, July 17, 2008. Online: http://www.archbishopofcanterbury.org/1914.

———. "The Archbishop's First Presidential Address." Lambeth Conference of the Anglican Communion, London, England, July 20, 2008. Online: http://www.archbishopofcanterbury.org/1898.

———. "The Archbishop's Second Presidential Address." Lambeth Conference of the Anglican Communion, London, England, July 29, 2008. Online: http://www.archbishopofcanterbury.org/1916.

———. "Concluding Presidential Address to the Lambeth Conference." Lambeth Conference of the Anglican Communion, London, England, August 3, 2008. Online: http://www.archbishopofcanterbury.org/1925

Witherington III, B. *Conflict and Community in Corinth: A Socio-Rhetorical Commentary on 1 and 2 Corinthians*. Carlisle: Paternoster, 1995.

Woolverton, J. F. *Colonial Anglicanism in North America*. Detroit: Wayne State University Press, 1984.

Young, P. "Church and State in the Legal Tradition of Australia " *Journal of Anglican Studies* 1 (2003) 92–118.